A Handbook of
Classroom English

Glyn S. Hughes

Oxford University Press

OXFORD
UNIVERSITY PRESS

Great Clarendon Street, Oxford OX2 6DP

Oxford University Press is a department of the University of Oxford.
It furthers the University's objective of excellence in research, scholarship,
and education by publishing worldwide in

Oxford New York

Auckland Cape Town Dar es Salaam Hong Kong Karachi
Kuala Lumpur Madrid Melbourne Mexico City Nairobi
New Delhi Shanghai Taipei Toronto

With offices in

Argentina Austria Brazil Chile Czech Republic France Greece
Guatemala Hungary Italy Japan Poland Portugal Singapore
South Korea Switzerland Thailand Turkey Ukraine Vietnam

OXFORD and OXFORD ENGLISH are registered trade marks of
Oxford University Press in the UK and in certain other countries

Typography, adaptation and additions © Oxford University Press 1981
Material reprinted from *Teacher Talk* © Glyn S. Hughes and Kustannusosakeyhtiö Otava,
Helsinki 1978

The moral rights of the author have been asserted

Database right Oxford University Press (maker)

First published 1981

2013 2012 2011 2010 2009
30 29 28 27 26 25 24 23 22 21

No unauthorized photocopying

ISBN : 978 0 19 431633 0

Printed in China

Not for sale in Finland

ACKNOWLEDGEMENTS

Illustrations on pages 88, 89, and 172 are from *Cartoons for Students of English 2* by Hill and
Mallet, published by Oxford University Press
All other cartoons are produced by kind permission of *Punch*

Contents

INTRODUCTION

Overall objectives

The aim of this book is to present and practise the language required by the teacher of English in the practical day-to-day management of classes. It is intended for two main groups of readers:

1 Trainee teachers. By working systematically through the materials in the book and applying them directly in the preparation of lesson plans, in micro-teaching sessions and actual demonstration lessons, students will acquire a wide range of accurate, authentic and idiomatic classroom phrases that will be of value throughout their teaching careers.

2 Teachers in the field. It is assumed that this group will already have attained a certain level of classroom competence, although experience suggests that there may be recurrent inaccuracies, or even an unwillingness to use English for classroom management purposes. It is hoped that this book will encourage experienced teachers to make more use of English and help them to extend the area of operation of their classroom English; for example, in running a language laboratory session in English.

The rather different needs of these two groups have meant that the format of the book is a compromise between a textbook and a work of reference.

Rationale

Teaching is considered primarily in terms of methodological problems and practical solutions to these problems. As a result teachers in training spend considerable time acquiring the basis of sound methodological habits for the presentation, practice and testing of learning items. It is, however, often forgotten that the classroom procedures derived from a particular method almost invariably have to be verbalized. In other words, instructions have to be given, groups formed, time limits set, questions asked, answers confirmed, discipline maintained, and so on. The role of this linguistic interaction is perhaps one of the least understood aspects of teaching, but it is clearly crucial to the success of the teaching/learning event.

Whatever the subject taught, all teachers require this specialized classroom competence and should be trained in it. Foreign language teachers in particular require linguistic training aimed at the classroom situation since, if they believe in the maximum use of the L2, that is, the language being taught, they are obliged to use it both as the goal of their teaching and as the prime medium of instruction and classroom management. Despite the linguistic demands of the L2 teaching situation, foreign language graduates are seldom adequately prepared for the seemingly simple task of running a class in the L2. The nature of the first-degree study programme may have meant that there was no opportunity to practise the key classroom functions of organization and interrogation, or teacher training units may be unwilling to interfere in what appears to be an aspect of 'knowledge of subject'. The result is generally that the trainee teacher acquires a very limited repertoire of classroom phrases, or makes as little use of the L2 as possible. In both cases there is likely to be a detrimental effect on learning:

'Our data indicate that teacher competence in the foreign language—however acquired—makes a significant difference in student outcomes. . . . The data appear to indicate that neither the sheer amount of teachers' university training in the foreign language, nor the amount of travel and residence in a foreign country, makes any particular difference in student outcomes. From the standpoint of teacher selection and training, this means that any measures taken that would increase teacher competence would have positive effects. . . .'

John B. Carroll,
The Teaching of French as a Foreign Language in Eight Countries.
(1975) pp. 277–8.

An extremely important element of overall teaching success is careful advance planning, but equally important is the teacher's flexibility in the actual classroom situation, i.e., the teacher's willingness and ability to deviate from a lesson plan, for example in order to make use of the pupils' own interests and suggestions, or to devote more time to individual learning difficulties. In the case of L2 teaching, such flexibility makes heavy demands on the teacher's foreign language skills, although the result may provide a learning bonus for the pupils:

'For the teaching of listening comprehension and spoken skills, more informal methods of language teaching are advisable—involving massive exposure of the student to the meaningful situational use of the language. One way of accomplishing this, our data strongly suggest, is to emphasize the use of the foreign language in the classroom, allowing the use of the mother tongue only where necessary to explain meanings of words and grammatical features of the language.'

The theoretical starting point of this book is that the classroom situation *is* a genuine social environment which allows 'the meaningful situational use of the language', and that its communicative potential is closer to real interaction than is often assumed. This view probably requires some further explanation:

1 Language is a tool and not a museum exhibit. As such one of its primary functions is to communicate information. In the classroom information gaps occur repeatedly, that is, the teacher has new information which the pupils require in order to continue participating in the lesson, or the pupils have answers which the teacher needs in order to know whether to proceed to the next stage of the lesson. These information gaps provide opportunities for language to be used communicatively. The phrase *'Open your books at page 10, please'* is not something the pupils repeat, translate, evaluate as true or false or put into the negative, but a genuine instruction which is followed by the simple action of opening a textbook. It is perhaps an interesting paradox that whereas teachers are quite willing to spend time practising key structures in phrases like *'Cows eat grass'* and *'Is John your mother?'*, they may well switch to the L1 in order to set the day's homework. The reason very often put forward for this is that the pupils may not understand! Any naive pupil may come to the very understandable conclusion that English is basically a very tedious subject since all the information it conveys is either known or meaningless. The instinctive reaction to a question like *'Who has got a grandmother?'*, for example, in the classroom situation is to repeat it, or answer it by reference to the text being dealt with. Only in the last resort will it be considered a personal question. Fortunately,

this kind of pedagogic ambiguity is usually avoided when the teacher adds the necessary functional label: 'No, I'm asking *you*.'

2 Much of the language put into the mouths of learners in the name of practice may well have little direct application outside the classroom, but many classroom management phrases can be transferred to 'normal' social situations, e.g. *Could you open the window*; *I'm sorry, I didn't catch that.* By using these phrases the teacher is demonstrating their contextualized use and indirectly accustoming the pupils to the form-function relationships (and discrepancies) that are part of English. Exposure to this aspect of language is particularly important in the case of polite requests (see p. 17).

3 Classroom situations and procedures are generally quite concrete, which means that most classroom phrases have a very clear situational link. This fact should allow the teacher to vary the form of the instructions given as part of the learning process. For example, given a specific context (repetition after the tape) which is familiar to the pupils, the teacher should be able to choose from '*All together*', '*The whole class*', '*Everybody*', '*Not just this row*', '*Boys as well*', '*In chorus*', or '*Why don't you join in?*' and the pupils should be able to react appropriately. In fact, by varying the phrases used in any particular situation, the teacher is giving the pupils a number of free learning bonuses. The pupil is hearing new vocabulary in context and at the same time developing the important skill of guessing the meaning of new words on the basis of the context. Similarly, the teacher can deliberately use a structure that is going to be taught actively in the coming lessons and so 'pre-expose' the pupils to it. For example, the future tense might be pre-exposed by choosing 'now we shall listen to a story' instead of 'let's listen'. Systematic variation is then a valuable pedagogic tool.

4 There still perhaps exists a belief that (i) pupils cannot really understand a sentence they hear unless they are able to break it up into separate words and explain the function of each of the words, and (ii) pupils at early stages should be able to say everything they hear in the lesson, and not hear anything that they are not able to say; in other words, there should be a 1:1 input–output ratio. This point of view implies that pupils at an elementary level would not understand '*Would you mind opening the door?*' and therefore they should not hear it since this type of structure occurs later in the textbook under the headings 'conditional' and 'gerund'. Clearly, however, the phrase '*Would you mind opening the door?*' can be understood in the simplest communicative sense on the basis of the key words '*open*' and '*door*'. The pupil may hear the '*Would you mind*' as a meaningless noise which will only be 'understood', i.e. broken up into its separate parts, later when the pupil has more experience of the language. If it is accepted that pupils may well understand more than they can say, it means that the teacher's choice of classroom phrases can exceed the pupils' productive abilities. This means, then, that the classroom can provide opportunities for the pupils to hear genuine uncontrolled language used for genuine communicative purposes. Because classroom activities are so diverse it is tempting to suggest that an entire teaching syllabus, even methodology, could be built around the use of classroom management phrases.

5 The classroom situation is often labelled 'artificial'. If artificiality can be measured statistically, it means that the 11 million schoolchildren in Britain spending 7 hours a day, five days a week, 40 weeks a year in school—a total of 15,400 million

hours!—are not engaged in some form of genuine social interaction, and, therefore, of course, the 50 million hours spent watching football matches is an even less genuine form of interaction. What in fact is meant by 'artificial' is that the interaction in the classroom is one-sided. For example, all exchanges are probably initiated by the teacher, or all pupil–pupil communication is mediated by the teacher. This obviously has something to do with the prestige position accorded to teachers traditionally, but in the case of language learning it may be due to the fact that pupils are not equipped from the outset with the necessary linguistic code, that is, the phrases and vocabulary related to their needs and problems as learners which would allow them to take part in the lesson as equals. By giving intermediate learners a list similar to that contained in Appendix 1 (p. 219), practising the phrases and then insisting on their use, the teacher is increasing the pupils' opportunities for using the language communicatively. After all, the teacher may well be the only living interacting source of the language and the classroom may well be the only social context for practising it. Even at an elementary level pupils can acquire classroom phrases holophrastically (i.e. as self-contained unchanging units), e.g. *I'm sorry I'm late*; *Could you repeat that*; *What's the answer to number 1?* The phrases used to talk about the language itself and learning it *Can you say that?*; *What's the English for this word?*; *Is there a corresponding adjective?*; etc., are particularly useful but seldom taught. Such metalinguistic phrases provide the pupils with a means of improving their language skills independently, that is, by asking native-speakers for corrections, explanations, etc.

Even though this book emphasizes the importance of making the maximum use of the L2 in the classroom situation for the benefit of the learners, it is not a dogmatic plea for a new monolingual teaching orthodoxy. When outlining new working methods or giving formal grammatical explanations, for example, teachers should feel free to use the L1. Naturally, an attempt can first be made in the L2, followed by an L1 translation. This method has the advantage of allowing for differentiation; that is, the better pupils have an opportunity to listen and try to understand while the weaker ones can rely more on the L1 translation. After all, successive translation is not unlike the subtitling used in films and television programmes which many pupils are accustomed to. The switching from language to language need not be a disturbing factor, especially if the teacher prefaces each change, e.g. *I'd like to say something in Spanish now*, *Let's use English now*. An alternative method is to appoint a class interpreter whose job it is to translate any unclear instructions. Experience suggests that pupils enjoy this, and it may be of practical value. Similarly, a pupil can be given the task of checking new or difficult words from a dictionary.

The main point should now be clear: the classroom situation, despite its renowned remoteness from real life, has enormous intrinsic potential in language teaching. By managing the class deliberately and flexibly in the L2, the teacher is taking an important step towards removing the barriers between controlled, and often meaningless, practice and more genuine interactional language use. In other words, the very goal of a teacher's efforts can also be used as a powerful and adaptable tool in achieving that goal.

Specific objectives

In the following list the various language functions related to classroom management have been grouped under key headings and expressed in terms of what the teacher should be able to do. The headings are suggestive only but they may be useful to Teacher Training Institutes in the preparation of syllabuses aimed at teaching classroom competence.

Language Functions Related to:	Objectives	Sample Phrases
A. ORGANIZATION		
A1. Giving Instructions.	The teacher gives appropriate instructions related to recurrent classroom activities, e.g. using textbooks, blackboard work, group work.	Open your books at page 73. Come out and write it on the board. Listen to the tape, please. Get into groups of four. Finish this off at home. Let's sing a song.
	The teacher can control the pupils' behaviour by means of commands, requests, and suggestions. Usage should correspond to native-speaker usage.[1]	*Could you* try the next one. *I would like you to* write this down. *Would you mind* switching the lights on. *It might be an idea* to leave this till next time.
	The teacher can vary the form of instructions in order to show the range of possibilities in the foreign language.	Everybody, please. All together, now. The whole class, please. I want you all to join in.
	The teacher can offer the pupils alternatives, i.e. different working methods, themes, groups.	Who would like to read? Which topic will your group report on? Do you want to answer question 6?
A2. Sequencing	The teacher can sequence the lesson effectively and communicate this sequencing to the pupils.	First of all today, . . . Right. Now we shall go on to exercise 2. All finished? O.K. For the last thing today, let's . . .
	The teacher can check what stage the pupils have reached, whose turn it is, and so on.	Whose turn is it to read? Which question are you on? Next one, please. Who hasn't answered a question yet?
	The teacher can introduce the class to a new activity and new stage of the lesson.	Let me explain what I want you to do next. The idea of this exercise is for you to make . . .
	The teacher can set time-limits related to various activities.	You have ten minutes to do this. Your time is up. Finish this by twenty to ten.
	The teacher can check that all pupils are equally capable of starting the next stage of the lesson.	Can you all see the board? Have you found the place? Are you all ready?

INTRODUCTION

Language Functions Related to:	Objectives	Sample Phrases
A3. Supervision	The teacher can direct pupils' attention to the lesson content.	Look this way. Stop talking. Listen to what Alan is saying. Leave it alone now!
	The teacher can give warnings and threats.	Be careful of the lead. One more word and . . .
B. INTERROGATION B1. Asking Questions	The teacher can ask questions fluently and flexibly, using the various forms available in the foreign language.[3]	Where's Alan? Is Alan in the kitchen? Tell me where Alan is.
	The teacher can ask questions related to specific communicative tasks, e.g. giving a description, opinion, reason, or stimulating conversation.	What was the house like? What do you think about this ' problem? Yes, but how can you tell?
B2. Replying to Questions	The teacher can give verbal confirmation of pupils' replies and/or guide them to the correct reply.	Yes, that's right. Fine. Almost. Try it again. What about this word here?
	The teacher can give encouraging feedback both in controlled drill-type exercises and freer conversation.	Very good. That's more like it. Could you explain what you mean?
C. EXPLANATION C1. Metalanguage	The teacher can produce and also get the pupils to produce a translation, a paraphrase, a summary, a definition, a correct spelling, a correct pronunciation and grammatical corrections.	What's the Swedish for 'doll'? Explain it in your own words. It's spelt with a capital 'J'. Can anybody correct this sentence?
	The teacher can give written and spoken instructions for exercises.	Fill in the missing words. Mark the right alternative.
C2. Reference	The teacher can give appropriate background factual information related to people, places and events.	After they left the USA in 1965, the Beatles . . . The church was started in the last century.
	The teacher can give a verbal commentary to accompany pictures, slides and films.	This is a picture of a typically English castle. In the background you can see . . .

Language Functions Related to:	Objectives	Sample Phrases
	The teacher can use basic rhetorical devices to make the commentary more interesting and more easily followed.	While we're on the subject of . . . As I said earlier, . . . Let me sum up then.
D. INTERACTION D1. Affective Attitudes	The teacher can express anger, interest, surprise, friendship, appreciation, pity, sympathy, disappointment, etc., as needed in the classroom situation.	That's interesting! That really is very kind of you. Don't worry about it. I was a bit disappointed with your results.
D2. Social Ritual	The teacher can use everyday phrases related to recurrent social situations, e.g. greeting, leaving, apologizing, thanking, congratulating, and other seasonal greetings.	Good morning. Cheerio now. God bless! Have a nice weekend. Thanks for your help. Happy birthday! Merry Christmas!

1. See Unit 1, page 13.
2. This is a good example of the way in which practical classroom methods are supported and reinforced by adequate language skills.
3. See Unit 2, page 33.

How to use the book

The material consists of 10 units. Units 1 and 2 deal in detail with the two main language functions related to classroom management, namely: giving instructions and asking questions. Units 3–10 constitute the core of the book and contain lists of classroom phrases grouped around key situations and activities.

Units 1–10 are constructed in the following way:

1. In the top left-hand corner of the left-hand page there is the number of the unit, the letter identifying the section and the title of the section; e.g. 9 L **Repetition and Responses**. On the right-hand page there is the number identifying the sub-section and its title; e.g. 2 GROUPING.

2. The actual phrases are grouped on the right-hand page under key sentences, given in bold type; e.g. **4 In turns**. This sentence or phrase acts as a point of reference. The phrases listed under it are usually variations or more difficult versions of the sentence, or phrases relating to the same context or activity;

   e.g. One after the other, please
   In turn, starting with Bill
   Take it in turns, starting here

The phrases are not graded in any way nor marked for their suitability at different levels. The choice made by teachers is a personal decision which will ultimately depend on their own methodological beliefs and practices.

The majority of the phrases involving instructions are given in the basic imperative form, although teachers are recommended (see above, page 9) to make use of the wide range of variations outlined in Unit 1, as and when appropriate.

11

Notice that certain phrases occur under different headings and that, since the list does not claim to be exhaustive, adequate space is left for teachers to add their own discoveries or pet usages.

3. The left-hand page contains comments and remarks (indicated ●) related to language use, grammar, vocabulary and pronunciation. Certain common errors (indicated ★) are also listed, together with their correct form. Notice that Standard British English has been used as a model.

   The cartoons scattered throughout the book are meant primarily for light relief, but they should also help when the book is used as a source of reference.

4. At the end of each unit there is a series of exercises with answers. These are mainly of four types: 1) Vocabulary and idiom; 2) structure and grammar; 3) activation of the unit materials, and 4) suggestions for micro-teaching topics. There has been no attempt to grade exercises precisely or systematically either within each unit or over the course of the whole book. Many of the superficially simple exercises are designed to expose the reader repeatedly to the classroom phraseologies.

Although the ten units were conceived of as an integrated whole, each one is self-contained and can be used separately. This allows the teacher or trainee to select his or her progression sequence. Once familiar with the main outline of the contents, the trainee can then use the book for reference purposes, for example, in the preparation of lesson plans. Inevitably, teachers will develop preferences for certain phrases, but the principle of variation mentioned above (p. 11) should be remembered.

The original version of the book was designed for Finnish trainee teachers and it is possible that the phrases selected reflect some of the methodological principles current in Finland. The material was collected on the basis of approximately 200 hours of English lessons at all levels in Finland, and 25 hours of teaching in an English comprehensive school. The book has been successfully used in Finnish Institutes of Education since 1978.

Unit 1

Getting Things Done in the Classroom
1.1 Commanding
1.2 Requesting
1.3 Suggesting and Persuading
Exercises
Answers

*'That's what I like about strolling in the park during my lunch-hour—
I get a marvellous sense of freedom when I get back to my office.'*

1 GETTING THINGS DONE IN THE CLASSROOM

A teacher has a number of alternative ways of controlling the behaviour of pupils. Perhaps the most important of these are 1) commands, 2) requests and 3) suggestions. Although in normal social interaction the selection from these alternatives is made quite carefully on the basis of factors related to status, role and situation, the choice in the classroom is often considered to be largely irrelevant. Because of the status traditionally accorded to the teacher and the situational rules that apply in the classroom, all of these different alternatives operate as commands, i.e. the pupil will do what he or she is told. Nevertheless, even within a clear-cut educational context, the choice may reflect the teacher's underlying attitude to the pupils. The use of commands emphasizes the teacher's position of authority; requests imply the notion of equality, and suggestions, at least in theory, allow the pupils some freedom of choice.

In order to see how closely the distribution of commands, requests and suggestions in the classroom situation reflected normal social usage, a small-scale investigation was carried out. The results are shown in Table 1 below:

	Situation 1	Situation 2	Situation 3
Commands (Imperatives, **must**)	85	50	10
Requests (Polite intonation, **please, could/would, mind**)	5	20	60
Suggestions (**let's, how about, why not, had better**)	10	30	30

Table 1: Percentage distribution of commands, requests and suggestions in three situations.

Situation 1: 10 English lessons given by graduate teacher trainees in Finnish secondary schools. Pupils aged 14–15.
Situation 2: 10 mother-tongue (English) and history lessons given by native-speaker trainee teachers in an English comprehensive school. Pupils aged 15–16.
Situation 3: 4 meals involving members of the family and guests. Total duration 9 hours.

Even on the basis of this very restricted data, and assuming that Finnish teachers are not exceptionally imperious, it seems reasonable to conclude that foreign learners of English are being given a distorted model in that the teacher's use of the suasive function of language neither corresponds with usage in a similar native-speaker situation nor with actual genuine use in social interaction. Where then is the learner to acquire these all-important language functions and the rules for their appropriate use if the teacher fails to use them? And what is the typical native-speaker reaction when the foreigner makes the incorrect choice? — 'rude', 'direct', 'bossy'? It is one of the ironies of language teaching that polite requests are taught as part of the syllabus (**could you . . ., would you mind . . . -ing . . .**) but are never in fact used by the teacher.

The purpose of this unit is to present some of the alternative ways of expressing commands, requests and suggestions, and at the same time to review some of the associated grammatical problems. The categorization is intuitive, and many readers may feel that certain items belong to other categories.

1.1. COMMANDING

1.1.1 The simplest form of command is the imperative:

> **Open** the window
> **Close** your books

1.1.2 The corresponding negative form (prohibiting):

> **Don't write** this down
> **Don't look** at the answers

1.1.3 The imperative can be personalized:

> **Alison, you try** number 2
> **You say** it, **Tom**
> **You boys, listen** now
> **Answer** it, **somebody**
> **Come** on, **everybody**

An inverted word order is incorrect: (★ indicates an incorrect form)

★ Alison, *try you* the next one.
★ *Say you* it, Tom.

1.1.4 The negative imperative can also be personalized:

> **Don't you help** him, **Mark**
> **Don't you talk, you two girls**
> **Don't anybody move**

1.1.5 An emphatic form of the imperative exists which expresses annoyance or frustration:

> **Do** be quiet now
> **Do** try to hurry up

Notice the following:

> If you **don't be** quiet, you can . . .

The word **just** at the beginning of a command also expresses annoyance or frustration:

> **Just sit** down and be quiet
> **Just put** that book away

It may also suggest that the task is a small one:

| **Just pass** me that book, Alan |
| **Just turn** the lights off |

1.1.6 The verbs **want, like, expect, prefer** and **insist** can also introduce commands. Notice the various patterns:

Object + infinitive

I want	you to	finish this off at home
I would like		try exercise 24A
I (would) prefer		use your own words
I expect		prepare down to page 35

Notice the two negative forms and the differences in their use:

I don't want you	to spend too much time on this
I wouldn't like you	to do this exercise in a hurry
I don't expect you	to write a masterpiece

I (would) prefer you	not to use a dictionary
I would like you	not to keep interrupting
I expect the boys	not to make any noise

Object + past participle

I want	this work (to be)	finished by Friday
I would like		copied out neatly
I (would) prefer		done in your notebooks
I expect		finished off at home

Gerund

| I prefer | you(r) | leaving out the easy ones |
| I insist on | | at least trying the exercise |

| I prefer | this work (being) | written out in full |
| I insist on | | done in groups |

'That' + verb phrase

| I prefer | (that) you | learn these words by heart |
| I insist | | use the passive |

Notice the errors:
★ I *want that* you . . .
★ I would *like that* you . . .
Verb phrase (imperfect)

I'd (I would)	prefer it if rather	you rewrote number 5 you did this at home

1.1.7   Commands can also be expressed by means of the modal auxiliaries **must, have to** and **should**:

> **You will have to** write this out again
> **You must** have this finished by Monday
> **You should** write your name at the top

The command can be weakened by adding **I'm afraid**:

> You must use the past tense here, **I'm afraid**
> **I'm afraid you will have to** do this again

1.1.8   The verb **to be** followed by 'to' + infinitive expresses an instruction:

> **You are to** work in groups of four
> **You are not to** talk
> **You are to** finish this off at home

1.2   REQUESTING

1.2.1   A command can be turned into a request by using a low rising intonation[1]:

Command	Request
Try it again, Bill ↘	Try it again, Bill ⤴
Come out here ↘	Come out here ⤴

1.2.2   A command can be turned into a request by adding the word **please**. This is probably the most frequent form of request. 'Please' can be placed at the beginning or end of the command:

Command	Request
Put your pencils down	Please put your pencils down ⤴
	Put your pencils down, please ⤴ ⤴

A request (low rising) intonation usually accompanies the use of 'please'.

---

1. The following intonation symbols are used: ↘ falling   ↗ high-rising   ⤴ low-rising.

If the name of a pupil is used as well, the order of the name and 'please' can vary. 'Please' before the verb, however, may sound more formal:

'Please' before verb	'Please' after verb
Tom, please come here	Tom, come here, please
Please, Tom, come here	Come here, please, Tom
Please come here, Tom	Come here, Tom, please

Notice that when several pupils put their hands up to answer and the teacher wants to select a particular pupil, he can do so using 'please':

Number 7. Yes, **Karen, please**
Right, the next one. Err, **Mohammed, please**

1.2.3 Want and like used in questions also express requests:

Would you like to write that on the board?
Do you want to try the next one?
Would anybody like to be the narrator?

1.2.4 One of the commonest forms of request in English involves the use of a modal auxiliary, **can, could, will** and **would**. Of these 'would' and 'could' are the politest.

Could you share with Anne today
Would you prepare chapter 24
Will you write this out neatly at home
Can you say that again

But notice:

★ **Who would say** that one?
★ **Who would write** it on the board?

1.2.5 Very frequently these forms are accompanied by **please**:

Could you **please** try question 5 at home
Would you come out to the front, **please**
Please will you try to remember your workbooks
Can you write that on the board, **please**

Notice that the position of 'please' varies, but it tends to come either before the infinitive or at the end of the sentence. Initial position is less common and more formal:

Could you **please** give these sheets out
Could you give these sheets out, **please**
Please could you give these sheets out

1.2.6 An extremely common variation involving the modal auxiliaries makes use of a tag-like ending:

> Clean the board, **would you**
> Try it again, **will you**
> Do number 6, **could you**
> Open the window, **can you**

If the word 'please' is also used it can occupy three positions:

> (1) look this way (2) could you (3)
> **Please** look this way, could you
> Look this way, **please,** could you
> Look this way, could you, **please**

Where the name of a pupil is also mentioned, the positions of name, tag and 'please' are freely interchangeable at the end of the sentence:

Open the window	could you, please, John
	John, could you, please
	please, John, could you
	could you, John, please
	please, could you, John
	John, please, could you

1.2.7 The following polite forms are also common. Notice the various forms of complementation:

> **Do you think you could** write this out at home?
> **I wonder if you could** say it in your own words
> **Would you mind** sharing today?
> **Do you mind** repeating what you said?

1.2.8 A number of super-polite forms also exist.

> **Would you be so kind as to** stop talking
> **Would you be kind enough to** lend me your copy

1.2.9 Despair, anger or frustration can be expressed by using the following phrases:

> **I wish** you **would** listen!
> **If only** you **would** try!
> **Can't** you **even** try?

1 GETTING THINGS DONE IN THE CLASSROOM

1.3 SUGGESTING AND PERSUADING

1.3.1 Perhaps the most frequent form of direct suggestion involves the use of **let's**.

> **Let's start** now
> **Let's finish** this off next time

'Let us' is archaic and should not be used.
Notice that there are two alternative forms of the negative:

> **Let's not waste** any more time
> **Don't let's bother** with number 10

This form of suggestion is very often accompanied by the tag ending **shall we**?
Notice that the tag is the same for positive and negative forms:

> **Let's try** the next exercise as well, **shall we**?
> **Let's not listen** to it again, **shall we**?
> **Don't let's do** all of exercise 5, **shall we**?

'Nurse, can you suggest a topic of conversation?'

1.3.2 Suggestions can also be made using **how about** or **what about** with a noun or a gerund:

> **How about** another song, children?
> **What about** trying it once more?
> **How about Bill** coming out and trying?
> **What about you** reading Mr Brown's part, Sally?

How about and what about can also be used when obtaining answers to questions:

> Number 9 then. **How about** that one, Pierre?
> OK, the next one. **How about** you, Yutaka?

1.3.3 A similar form of suggestion makes use of **what if** and a verb phrase. The verb may be either in the present or past, although modern usage seems to prefer the present, especially where the function is clearly that of suggestion and not question:

> **What if we leave** this exercise until next time?
> **What if you finish** this off at home?

> **What if we change(d)** the word order?
> **What if you start(ed)** with 'Yesterday'?
> **What if you (were to) put** the verb at the end?

Colloquially, it is possible to use **what about if** and **how about if** in the same way:

> **What about if** we translate these sentences?
> **How about if** you start(ed) with the adverb?

1.3.4 The questions **why not, why don't we** and **couldn't we** can be used as suggestions:

> **Why not leave** the adverb until the end?
> **Why don't we** act this conversation out?
> **Couldn't we say** this in a simpler way?

1.3.5 Notice that the teacher can soften a command by using **I think, don't you think?** and **perhaps**:

> **I think** we ought to revise these points
> **I think** you should concentrate on number 3
>
> Number 6 can be left out, **don't you think**?
> We can finish this next time, **don't you think**?
>
> **Perhaps** you ought to translate this paragraph
> You could check the vocabulary at the back **perhaps**

1.3.6 A direct suggestion can be introduced by the phrases **I suggest, I would suggest, may I suggest** and **my suggestion is**. Notice the forms of complementation:

Gerund

I suggest I would suggest May I suggest	leaving this until next time starting with the verb appointing a secretary

Verb phrase

I suggest I would suggest May I suggest My suggestion is	(that)	you omit the relative we check this next time you learn these by heart you underline this phrase

Object + infinitive

My suggestion is	for you	to finish this off at home

After 'I would suggest' the verb may also be in the past:

I would suggest you cop**ied** this out again
I would suggest you **went** through this carefully

1.3.7 The verbs **may, can** and **need** can function as suggestions in the classroom situation:

You may sit down again now
You can leave question 8 out
You needn't do the first three

Notice the alternative patterns with **need**:

There's no need to translate everything
There's no need for you to do number 5

1.3.8 Phrases based around the word **idea** are often used to introduce suggestions. Notice the forms of complementation and the use of the past tense:

It might be an (good) idea It would be an (good) idea It mightn't be a bad idea It wouldn't be a bad idea	**to try** this one again **for you to** write this down **if you did** this at home

1.3.9 Notice the following phrases using **as well** or **just as well** and the modal auxiliaries **can, may** and **would**:

We may as well leave this exercise till Tuesday
You might as well leave number 4 out

> **We can just as well** use the continuous here
> **You could just as well** leave the 'that' out
> **We might just as well** stop here this time

> **It would be just as well to** check this at home
> **It would be just as well for you to** revise this

1.3.10 Advice used to persuade often takes the form of a conditional:

It would be	better quicker neater		if you	wrote in ink just crossed the word underlined it
	more	English sensible	to	begin 'Who did . . .' listen in sections

Better is also used in the following phrase:

> **You'd** (= you had) **better** do this exercise again

It is incorrect to say:
★ You'd better *to* listen.

1.3.11 Notice the use of **rather** in the following examples:

> **I'd rather you finished** this off at home
> **I'd rather you didn't look** at the answers yet

Exercises

I. In each of the sets of four sentences below it is possible to make one or n.
grammatically correct instructions by choosing an appropriate form of
complementation. Read out the correct instructions.

Example:
a) Don't let's — 1) translate the whole text
b) Why not — 2) to translate the whole text
c) I prefer —
d) How about —

Answer:
a) *1*
b) *1*
c) *2*
d) —

1. a) I insist on you — 1) to finish this off at home
   b) I want you — 2) finish this off at home
   c) I suggest you —
   d) Why not —

2. a) Would you mind — 1) to leave out the next one
   b) How about — 2) leave out the next one
   c) It would be a good idea —
   d) Do you mind —

3. a) What if — 1) to start with the adverb
   b) Why not — 2) start with the adverb
   c) There's no need —
   d) I'd prefer you —

4. a) I suggest — 1) you don't keep forgetting your books
   b) I would like — 2) you wouldn't keep forgetting your books
   c) I wish —
   d) I want —

5. a) What if — 1) this exercise to be done at home
   b) I prefer — 2) do the exercise at home
   c) It might be an idea for —
   d) There's no need for —

6. a) My suggestion is — 1) for you to check the answers on your own
   b) I insist — 2) you checking the answers on your own
   c) I'd rather —
   d) I expect —

7. a) Don't let's — 1) spend a lot of time on number 9
   b) You needn't — 2) to spend a lot of time on number 9
   c) I prefer you not —
   d) I think you should —

8. a) Would you mind — 1) working on your own
   b) What if you, Bill, — 2) work on your own
   c) I'd prefer you —
   d) Would you be so kind as —

9. a) There's no need — 1) try the next exercise
   b) Why not — 2) for you to try the next exercise
   c) I would like —
   d) What about —

10. a) What if we — 1) starting from the middle of page 23
    b) Don't let's — 2) start from the middle of page 23
    c) I wish you —
    d) I suggest you —

11. a) Would you be so kind as to — 1) read out your answer to question 10
    b) Do you mind — 2) reading out your answer to question 10
    c) I insist on you —
    d) You needn't —

12. a) What if you — 1) putting a different preposition at the end
    b) I prefer — 2) put a different preposition at the end
    c) Why not —
    d) I would suggest —

13. a) It would be just as well — 1) for you to revise chapter 6 as well
    b) It might be an idea — 2) you to revise chapter 6 as well
    c) I expect —
    d) I would like —

14. a) I'd prefer it if — 1) this work were finished off at home
    b) I suggest — 2) on this work being finished off at home.
    c) I insist —
    d) What if —

15. a) I'd rather — 1) to go on to the next exercise
    b) I want you — 2) go on to the next exercise
    c) You had better —
    d) You might as well —

16. a) You had better — 1) use the past tense in number 7
    b) I would like you — 2) to use the past tense in number 7
    c) You can just as well —
    d) Why not —

17. a) I insist on you — 1) writing out the whole of what Smith says
    b) Do you mind — 2) to write out the whole of what Smith says
    c) I expect you —
    d) You had better —

18. a) I'd rather — 1) you not to look up the answers just yet
    b) What if — 2) you wouldn't look up the answers just yet
    c) I'd prefer —
    d) I wish —

II. Rewrite the following instructions, making use of the clue words given in brackets.

Example: | Finish exercise 7 at home. (I want)
I want you to finish exercise 7 at home. |

1 EXERCISES

1. Repeat what you said. (Do you think … could)
2. Translate the whole of paragraph 3 (not a bad idea … you …)
3. Start with the preposition. (I suggest)
4. Go and sit next to Julie. (Do you mind?)
5. Come out and write in on the board. (I would like)
6. Make a note of this somewhere. (I think … should)
7. Tell Björn what you just said. (I wonder … could)
8. Don't use your dictionaries. (I prefer … not)
9. Try a little harder, Iman! (If only)
10. Don't look at the answers yet. (no need)

11. Let's only do every other question. (May I suggest)
12. Listen carefully to what I say. (Could)
13. You try number 7, John. (How about)
14. Don't bother reading the introduction. (Let's)
15. This essay will be finished by Friday. (I expect)
16. Begin your sentence with 'when'. (Why not)
17. Read the part of Alice, girls. (I want)
18. Give out the listening tests. (kind enough)
19. Prepare up to page 56 by Monday. (are to)
20. Pay attention, Sue! (I wish)

21. The answers should be written out in full. (I prefer)
22. Read out what you wrote, too, Dimitri. (might be an idea)
23. Let's have another look at the passage. (What if)
24. You join group 3, Françoise. (I would suggest)
25. Put that magazine in your desk. (be so kind)
26. Refer to the grammar section when doing the exercise. (better)
27. Leave number 3 until last. (prefer it if)
28. Spend some time revising the use of the article. (be just as well)
29. Copy this straight off the board. (might as well)
30. Don't use more than 150 words in your summary. (rather)

III. Activating Drills. Change each of the following sets of sentences according to the example. Cover the answers with a piece of paper, etc., until you have attempted to answer yourself.

A) Answer: | Shall we act this out? (just read it)
No, let's not act this out.
How about just reading it **instead**. |

1. Shall we try exercise 9 as well? (try something more difficult)
   No, let's not try exercise 9 as well.
   How about trying something more difficult instead?
2. Shall we work in pairs? (work in threes or fours)
   No, let's not work in pairs.
   How about working in threes or fours instead?
3. Shall we listen with our books open? (try it on your own)
   No, let's not listen with our books open.
   How about trying it on your own instead?

4. Shall we finish this off now? (leave it until next time)
   No, let's not finish this off now.
   How about leaving it until next time instead?
5. Shall we continue with chapter 8? (go through last week's test)
   No, let's not continue with chapter 8.
   How about going through last week's test instead?
6. Shall we play a guessing game again? (sing 'London Town).
   No, let's not play a guessing game again.
   How about singing 'London Town' instead?

B) Example: | Leave out number 7. (number 9)
   I want you to leave out number 7.
   And what if you leave out number 9 **as well**? |

1. Learn the vocabulary on page 76. (page 77)
   I want you to learn the vocabulary on page 76.
   And what if you learn the vocabulary on page 77 as well?
2. Underline all the conditional verbs. ('If's')
   I want you to underline all the conditional verbs.
   And what if you underline all the 'if's as well?
3. Translate the last but one sentence. (the last sentence)
   I want you to translate the last but one sentence.
   And what if you translate the last sentence as well?
4. Prepare the first three chapters. (half of chapter 4)
   I want you to prepare the first three chapters.
   And what if you prepare half of chapter 4 as well?
5. Finish off exercise 12A on page 118. (start exercise 12B)
   I want you to finish off exercise 12A on page 118.
   And what if you start exercise 12B as well?
6. Learn the words of the song by heart. (the extra vocabulary)
   I want you to learn the words of the song by heart.
   And what if you learn the extra vocabulary by heart as well?

C) Example: | Speak more quietly. (make no noise at all)
   Would you mind speaking more quietly?
   I'd prefer you to make no noise at all, **though**. |

1. Share with Bill this time. (bring your own book)
   Would you mind sharing with Bill this time?
   I'd prefer you to bring your own book, though.
2. Write what you said on the board. (start with 'He said')
   Would you mind writing what you said on the board?
   I'd prefer you to start with 'He said', though.
3. Go and sit next to Alan. (not sit right at the back)
   Would you mind going and sitting next to Alan?
   I'd prefer you not to sit right at the back, though.
4. Read your question out again. (stand up and speak louder)
   Would you mind reading your question out again?
   I'd prefer you to stand up and speak louder, though.

5. Translate the next line as well. (start with the adverb)
   Would you mind translating the next line as well?
   I'd prefer you to start with the adverb, though.
6. Listen carefully to Jussi's question. (not write it down this time)
   Would you mind listening carefully to Jussi's question?
   I'd prefer you not to write it down this time, though.

D) Example: | Try number 7. (Bill) (Tim)
Try number 7, **could you, please**, Bill.
No? **I wonder if you could** try number 7, **then**, Tim. |

1. Give me a good English translation of this sentence. (Paul) (Chieko)
   Give me a good English translation of this sentence, could you, please, Paul.
   No? I wonder if you could give me a good English translation of this sentence, then, Chieko.
2. Read out the correct answer to number 2. (Li) (Delma)
   Read out the correct answer to number 2, could you, please, Li.
   No? I wonder if you could read out the correct answer to number 2, then, Delma.
3. Give me the noun that comes from 'compose'. (Kurt) (Anita)
   Give me the noun that comes from 'compose', could you, please, Kurt.
   No? I wonder if you could give me the noun that comes from 'compose', then, Anita.
4. Start summarizing what the stranger said (Federico) (Zoran)
   Start summarizing what the stranger said, could you, please, Federico.
   No? I wonder if you could start summarizing what the stranger said, then Zoran.
5. Tell us the main rules for using 'no' and 'none'. (Maria) (Marco)
   Tell us the main rules for using 'no' and 'none', could you, please, Maria.
   No? I wonder if you could tell us the main rules for using 'no' and 'none', then, Marco.
6. Translate the final sentence in paragraph 2. (Erik) (Per)
   Translate the final sentence in paragraph 2, could you, please, Erik.
   No? I wonder if you could translate the final sentence in paragraph 2, then, Per.

E) Example: | Repeat your answer.
Do you think you could repeat your answer?
I'm afraid you'll have to repeat it again. |

1. Read out what you wrote for number 2.
   Do you think you could read out what you wrote for number 2?
   I'm afraid you'll have to read it out again.
2. Mention the exceptions to this rule.
   Do you think you could mention the exceptions to this rule?
   I'm afraid you'll have to mention them again.
3. Try the next question.
   Do you think you could try the next question?
   I'm afraid you'll have to try it again.
4. Translate the last two lines.
   Do you think you could translate the last two lines?
   I'm afraid you'll have to translate them again.
5. Say what you put for the last one.
   Do you think you could say what you put for the last one?
   I'm afraid you'll have to say it again.

6. Repeat the answer to number 5.
Do you think you could repeat the answer to number 5?
I'm afraid you'll have to repeat it again.

F) Example: | Revise chapter 11. (chapter 10)
It would be as well for you to revise chapter 11.
And it wouldn't be a bad idea if you revised chapter 10, **too.** |

1. Translate lines 3 to 5. (the last sentence)
It would be as well for you to translate lines 3 to 5.
And it wouldn't be a bad idea if you translated the last sentence, too.
2. Go through these sentences again at home. (those on page 76)
It would be as well for you to go through these sentences again at home.
And it wouldn't be a bad idea if you went through those on page 76, too.
3. Look up the meaning of these words. (the new words in chapter 15)
It would be as well for you to look up the meaning of these words.
And it wouldn't be a bad idea if you looked up the meaning of the new words in chapter 15, too.
4. Answer the first two questions while listening. (question 7)
It would be as well for you to answer the first two questions while listening.
And it wouldn't be a bad idea if you answered question 7 while listening, too.
5. Underline the sentences containing gerunds. (infinitives with 'to')
It would be as well for you to underline the sentences containing gerunds.
And it wouldn't be a bad idea if you underlined the sentences containing infinitives with 'to', too.
6. Spend some time practising these forms. (the irregular verbs)
It would be as well for you to spend some time practising these forms.
And it wouldn't be a bad idea if you spent some time practising the irregular verbs, too.

G. Example: | Do this at home. (down to page 34)
There's no need to do this all at home.
I suggest you do **down to page 34.** |

1. Underline the passives. (just those on page 16)
There's no need to underline all the passives.
I suggest you underline just those on page 16.
2. Read chapter 6 at home. (as far as 'And was dead')
There's no need to read all chapter 6 at home.
I suggest you read as far as 'And was dead'.
3. Do the vocabulary exercise on page 20. (questions 1–6)
There's no need to do all the vocabulary exercise on page 20.
I suggest you do questions 1–6.
4. Rewrite your essay. (the sentences containing mistakes)
There's no need to rewrite all your essay.
I suggest you rewrite the sentences containing mistakes.
5. Prepare the next chapter. (up to line 24, page 56)
There's no need to prepare all the next chapter.
I suggest you prepare up to line 24, page 56.

6. Check the spelling of these words. (just the ones you're not sure of)
   There's no need to check the spelling of all these words.
   I suggest you check just the ones you're not sure of.

ANSWERS

I.

1. a) —	2. a) —	3. a) —	4. a) 1	5. a) —	6. a) 1
b) 1	b) —	b) 2	b) —	b) 1	b) —
c) 2	c) 1	c) 1	c) 2	c) 1	c) —
d) 2	d) —	d) 1	d) —	d) 1	d) —

7. a) 1	8. a) 1	9. a) 2	10. a) 2	11. a) 1	12. a) 2
b) 1	b) 2	b) 1	b) 2	b) 2	b) 1
c) 2	c) 1	c) —	c) —	c) 2	c) 2
d) 1	d) —	d) —	d) 2	d) 1	d) 1

13. a) 1	14. a) 1	15. a) 1	16. a) 1	17. a) 1	18. a) —
b) 1	b) —	b) 1	b) 2	b) 1	b) —
c) 2	c) 2	c) 2	c) 1	c) 2	c) 1
d) 2	d) 1	d) 2	d) 1	d) —	d) 2

II. Alternative correct answers are given in brackets:

1. Do you think you could repeat what you said?
2. It mightn't (wouldn't) be a bad idea for you to translate (if you translated) the whole of paragraph 3.
3. I suggest starting (you start) with the preposition.
4. Do you mind going and sitting next to Julie?
5. I would like you to come out and write it on the board.
6. I think you should (ought to) make a note of this somewhere.
7. I wonder if you could tell Björn what you just said.
8. I prefer you not to use (you not using) your dictionaries.
9. If only you would try a little harder, Iman!
10. There's no need (for you) to look at the answers yet.

11. May I suggest only doing (that we only do) every other question.
12. Could you listen carefully to what I say. (Listen carefully to what I say, could you.)
13. How about (you) trying number 7, John?
14. Let's not (Don't let's) bother reading the introduction.
15. I expect this essay (to be) finished by Friday.
16. Why not (Why don't you) begin your sentence with 'when'?
17. I want you to read the part of Alice, girls.
18. Would you be kind enough to give out the listening tests.
19. You are to prepare up to page 56 by Monday.
20. I wish you would pay attention, Sue!

21. I prefer the answers (to be) written out in full.
22. It might be an idea for you to read out (if you read out) what you wrote, too, Dimitri.
23. What if we have another look at the passage?
24. I would suggest that you join (joined) (you joining) group 3, Françoise.
25. Would you be so kind as to put that magazine in your desk.
26. You had better refer (It would be better if you referred) to the grammar section when doing the exercise.

27. I'd prefer it if you left number 3 until last.
28. It would be just as well for you to spend some time revising the use of the article.
29. You might as well copy this straight off the board.
30. I'd rather you didn't use more than 150 words in your summary.

*'You realise, of course, that failing your English
"O" level means saying goodbye to a career as a
T-shirt slogan writer?'*

Unit 2

Asking Questions

'*No!*'

2 ASKING QUESTIONS

2.1 PURPOSE OF QUESTIONS

Question-asking takes up a large proportion of the teacher's time. The questions the teacher asks can be roughly divided into two types:
(i) questions to which the teacher can provide the answer, although the pupils are initially expected to supply it;
(ii) questions to which the pupils alone can provide the answer.

Examples of the first type are:

2.1.1 Language questions (see Unit 10)

e.g. What's the past tense of 'to sing'?
Is this right?
What's the answer to number 6?

2.1.2 Comprehension questions

e.g. What is Mrs Lane doing in picture 1?
When does Mr Mason go to work?
What number is John?

Examples of the second type are:

2.1.3 Lesson progress questions (see Unit 9, pp. 181 ff.).

e.g. Has everybody got a book?
Are you ready?
Can you all see?

2.1.4 Opinion/preference questions

e.g. What did you think of the song?
Do you agree with Tim?
Who is your favourite singer?

A fifth group of questions also exists where it is not clear whether the teacher is asking because he does not know the answer and is interested, or whether the question merely rehearses an everyday situation:

2.1.5 Factual/personal questions

e.g. How are you today, Mark?
Have you any brothers or sisters?
What is the date today?

It is probably true to say that comprehension questions (group 2) predominate in the language classroom. Since these questions may well be improvised on the basis of an unfamiliar text, there is some likelihood of error. Experience also suggests that question-asking is a source of recurrent difficulty. The following sections review some of the main question types and the associated grammatical problems.

2.2   'Yes–No' QUESTIONS

2.2.1   Basic form

Auxiliary verb	Subject	Main verb	(Complement)
Is	it	raining?	—
Does	Ben	like	ice-cream?
Can	Bill	play	football?

NB: These questions require a high-rising intonation on the item being asked about:

Can Bill play **foot**ball?

Can **Bill** play football?

2.2.2   Negative questions

Isn't	it	raining?	—
Doesn't	Ben	like	ice-cream?
Can't	Bill	play	football?

NB: a) These questions may often suggest surprise or disbelief.
  b) The contracted or reduced form of the verb must be used. The same applies to negative questions beginning with a WH-word (**who**, **why**, **how**, etc.). The following are incorrect:
    ★ *Is not* it raining?
    ★ *Does not* Ben like ice-cream?
    ★ *Cannot* Bill play football?
  c) An alternative form also exists, but it is considered somewhat formal:

Is it not raining?
Does Ben not like ice-cream?
Can Bill not play football?

2.2.3   Rebound questions

Where a pupil answers a question and the teacher wishes to indicate that the answer is wrong and at the same time get a corrected answer, the following very common form may be useful:

Pupil: Mr Brown lives in London.
Teacher: Does he? / Mr Brown lives in London, does he?

The same purpose is served by phrases such as:

Are you sure?
Have another look.
Do you really think so? etc.

2.2.4 Replies to 'Yes–No' questions

In theory, pupils may answer 'Yes-no' questions in at least five ways:
1) Yes, . . .
2) No, . . .
3) Perhaps; well; maybe.
4) I don't know; I can't remember.
5) You must be joking!; what do you think?, etc.

In practice, however, their choice tends to be restricted to 'yes' and 'no'.
Notice that several equally acceptable 'Yes-No' replies are available:

Question: Is Bill English?
Answer: Yes
Yes, he is
Yes, he's English
Yes, Bill's English   But: ★ Yes, *he's*.

Question: Is Pekka English?
Answer: No
No, he isn't
No, he's not
No, he isn't English
No, he's not English
No, Finnish
No, he's Finnish
No, he isn't English; he's Finnish
No, he's Finnish, not English

2.3 'OR' QUESTIONS

2.3.1 Form

'Or' questions can take any of four forms:

1) Basic form—alternatives adjacent

> Is Peter Jones **eighteen or nineteen**?
> Does she take **cream or milk** in her coffee?
> Do you **watch TV or play tennis** at weekends?
> Did **Mr Mason or Mr Brown** buy the book?

2) Postponed form—2nd alternative at end

> Does she take **cream** in her coffee **or milk**?
> Do you **watch TV** at weekends **or play tennis**?
> Did **Mr Mason** buy the book **or (did) Mr Brown**?

3) Expanded form—2nd alternative in own verb phrase

> Is Peter Jones **eighteen or is he nineteen**?
> Does she take **cream** in her coffee **or does she take milk**?
> Do you **watch TV** at weekends **or do you play tennis**?
> Did **Mr Mason** buy the book **or did Mr Brown buy it**?

4) WH-form—both alternatives at end

> **How old** is Peter Jones, **eighteen or nineteen**?
> **What** does she take in her coffee, **cream or milk**?
> **What** do you do at weekends, **watch TV or play tennis**?
> **Who** bought the book, **Mr Mason or Mr Brown**?

NB: a) In the list of alternatives, the first item(s) are spoken on a high-rising (Yes-No) intonation, but the final item is on a falling intonation:

> Are the boys playing **foot**ball or **ice**-hockey?
> Who is in the shop, **John, Al**ice or **Bill**?

b) 'Yes-No' questions can be turned into 'or' questions by adding **or not**?:

> Is Ben **fond** of ice-cream or **not**?

Notice that if the question is said as a single tone group, the intonation is high-rising:

> Would you like to **try** it or not?

c) Where the items in the list are not real alternatives but meant as clues to guide the pupils, a rising intonation is used on the final item as well:

> What has Ben got? Well, has he got a **bicycle**, or a **pen**, or a **book**?

d) Where the teacher does not want to mention a particular alternative, but nevertheless help the pupil towards the correct answer, the second alternative can be **or something**:

> Well, does he feel **tired** or something?

'Or something' is not made into a separate tone group and continues the rising movement of the first alternative.

2.4 WH-QUESTIONS

2.4.1 Basic form

Basic question words:

> who, whom, whose
> what, which
> when, where, how
> why

Question word	Auxiliary verb	Subject	Main verb
Where	does	John	live?
When	is	Joan	leaving?
What	can	Ben	do?

NB: a) Normally, WH-questions are spoken on a falling intonation. A low
  rising intonation, however, indicates friendliness, encouragement,
  etc.

  b) A question like 'What is Ben?' would normally produce an answer

What is Ben?	He's a civil engineer
	He's managing director
	He's a Capricorn

But: ★ *He's a boy.*
  ★ *He's happy.*

  c) In negative WH-questions, the verb must appear in its contracted
  form:

Why can't he play football?
What haven't the boys done?

2.4.2   Longer WH-questions

Many WH-questions related to time, place and manner can be formed using
prepositions. Modern English usage tends to place the preposition at the
end of the question, but in several cases the preposition has disappeared
altogether. On the other hand, certain phrases require the preposition to be
in first position. In the following list, brackets around both prepositions
indicate that the preposition is optional.

1) Time

(In) **which year** were you born (in)?
(In) **which month** are they leaving (in)?
(On) **which day** will you phone (on)?
(On) **what date** does it start (on)?
(At) **what time** do we arrive (at)?
(For) **how long** (a time) will she stay (for)?
(For) **what length of time** is it valid (for)?
(At) **what** age can you marry (at)?
How often does he play football?
How many times (a week) do they play?
Since when has he been smoking?

2) Place

Whereabouts in London does he work?
Where are you going (to)?
Where are you coming **from**?
(From) **which part** of England is he **from**?
How far (away) is the nearest station?
Which way did the man go?
(In) **which direction** are they going (in)?

3) Manner

> **In what way** does this help?
> **To what extent** was he right?
> **Under what circumstances** would you do it?

2.4.3 Echo questions

If the teacher does not hear a reply or is surprised at it, the echo WH-question can be used:

> Teacher: How old is **Bill**?
>
> ↓
>
> Pupil: Ten
> Teacher: Pardon? **How** old is he?
>
> ↗

NB: a) In the echo question, the WH-word is emphasized.
      b) The intonation is high-rising.

2.4.4 'Else' and 'other'

Not: ★ *Where* have they been, *too*?
      ★ *What* books has he read, *too*?
      ★ *Which* animals live in Africa, *too*?

But: **Where else** have they been?
      What other books has he read?
      Which other animals live in Africa?

NB: Where the **too** refers to the subject of the sentence and not to the WH-word, 'too' is acceptable but may be replaced by **how about**? or **then**:

> Teacher: Ann is eating ice-cream
>   What is **Ben** eating, **too**?
>   And how about **Ben**?
>   What is **Ben** eating, then?
> Pupil: **He** is eating ice-cream, too

2.4.5 Subject questions

Where the WH-word refers to the subject of the sentence, the word order is **not** inverted:

WH-word Subject	Main verb	Complement Adverb
Who	lives	in Egypt?
What	frightened	the mouse?
Which runner	won	the race?
Whose car	span	off the track?
How many people	watched	it happen?
How much money	disappeared	in the robbery?

Note the possible replies to a subject question:

Question: Who arrived late?
Answer: The boys
          The boys did
          The boys arrived late

But: ★ The boys *arrived*.
     ★ The boys *did arrive late*.

Question: Who wanted the book?
Answer: Me
          I did
          I wanted it

But: ★ I *wanted*.
     ★ I *did want*.

Short answers of this sort are part of everyday usage and they should not be discouraged.

2.4.6 Non-reducible forms

Modern usage permits the extensive use of a reduced form of the verb after WH-question words:

What's he doing?
Where've you been?
What'd they been doing?

Where the question, however, contains only the WH-word and a pronoun, and the question word is emphasized, no reduction is possible:

This is Bill. ★ *Where*'s he?
This is Ann. ★ *What*'s she?
I have a present. ★ *What*'s it?

If the pronoun is emphasized, such forms are possible, except in the case of **it**, which is not usually emphasized through intonation. Generally it becomes **this** or **that**:

> Number 7. What's that in English   Not: ★ What's *it* in English?
> The last question. You try this one, Alain.   Not: ★ You try *it*.

2.4.7 Preposition questions

> What did he open the door **with**?
> Which line did we stop **at**?
> Which book did you look it up **in**?

NB: a) In sentences like the above, modern usage prefers to leave the preposition until the end.

b) If in the learner's native language the idea of the preposition is already contained in the question word, there is a danger that the corresponding preposition in English is omitted:

  ★ *What did he open the door?*
  ★ *Which line did we stop?*
  ★ *Which book did you look it up?*

c) Whom becomes **who** when the preposition is moved to final position:

> For whom did you do it? ⇒ Who did you do it for?

2.4.8 Passive questions

Where the WH-question refers to the agent in a passive sentence, some learners tend to omit the preposition *by*, which generally takes final position:

> Who wrote the book? ⇒ Who was the book written by?

But: ★ *Who was the book written?*
Where the passive consists of a single word only in the learner's language, there is a tendency to use the English equivalent in a similar way.

★ *What is called this book?*
instead of: **What is this book called**?

2.4.9 Quantity questions

a lot of	(a) little	least
many	(a) few	enough
much	too little	more than enough
more	too few	none
most	less	any

Questions based on the above expressions of quantity and on any cardinal number or fraction require a partitive **of** after the expression of quantity:

He had too much money—What did he have too much **of**?
They bought three ties—What did they buy three **of**?
We haven't any bread—What haven't we any **of**?

2.4.10   Questions about weight, age, colour, etc.

1) Size and dimension

In general there is a nominal and an adjectival form related to size and dimension:

How	**big**	is it?	=	What	**size**	is it?
	tall				**height** [hait]	
	high				**height**	
	long				**length**	
	deep				**depth**	
	thick				**thickness**	
	wide				**width**	
	broad				**breadth**	

Both forms can also function in adjectival phrases. Notice the use of the indefinite article:

How big **a** packet?	=	What size packet?
How tall **a** man?		What height man?
How high **a** mountain?		What height mountain?
etc.		etc.

Replies to these questions also use a nominal and adjectival form:

He is 1 m 90 tall
His height is 1 m 90
He is 1 m 90 **in** height

2) Weight

Notice the additional verbal form:

How heavy is it?
What weight is it?
What | does it weigh?
How much |

3) Shape and colour

No adjectival form exists:

What shape is the parcel? = What shape parcel?
What colour is her dress? = What colour dress?

4) Age

Adjectival and nominal forms exist:

> How old is Bill? = What age is Bill?
> How old a car do you want? = What age car?

Notice the replies:

> Bill is five (years old)
> Bill is five years of age

But not: ★ Bill is five *years*.

5) Type

Notice the additional **of** required in these questions:

> **What make of** car do you drive?
> **What brand of** toothpaste do you use?
> **What kind of** books?
> **What sort of** aeroplane was it?

But: ★ What *mark* of car is this?

6) Miscellaneous

Notice the following:

> **What time** train did they take?
> **What price** records are you interested in?
> **How many marks' worth of** cheese do you want?
> **What distance** did you have to walk?
> **What percentage of** the students voted?
> **What number bus** did they take?

2.5   INDIRECT QUESTIONS

2.5.1   Word order

If the question is made indirect, i.e. preceded by the phrases listed below, there is a change in the word order:

| Where **is he** going? ⇒ | Do you know
Can you tell me
Does anybody know | where **he is** going? |
| What **does Bill like**? ⇒ | Can anyone explain
Could you explain
Tell me
Try to describe
Have you any idea | what Bill **likes**? |

Mistakes persist in this area:

★ Tell me what *did he open* the door with?

★ Does anybody know *what's in* French 'snore'?

★ Do you know *what does this mean*?

2.5.2 'Do you think'

A similar change in word order takes place when the following phrases follow the question word:

> . . . do you think . . .
> . . . did you say . . .
> . . . would you say . . .
> . . . do you imagine . . .
> . . . would you guess . . .
> etc.

Where **is he** going? ⇒	Where do you think	**he is** going?
What **was he** doing? ⇒	What did you say	**he was** doing?
Why **did he** leave? ⇒	Why do you imagine	**he left**?

NB: The WH-word must not be repeated:

★ *What* do you think *where* is he going?

★ *What* do you think *how* old is she?

2.5.3 'Yes–No' questions

'Yes–No' questions can be made indirect by using **if** or **whether**, where necessary. The word order is changed:

| Is he fond of cake? | Do you know | if | he is fond of cake(?) |
| Does he like ice-cream? | Tell me | whether | he likes ice-cream(?) |

2.6. QUESTIONS ON SPECIFIC TEXTS

2.6.1 Asking for a description

| What is ice-cream like? | Ice-cream is nice |
| What is the book like? | It is interesting |

N.B.: a) **Like** may precede any relative clause, but is often found in final position, even after fairly long relatives:

> What was the book **like** you bought last week?
> What was the book you bought last week **like**?

b) Notice the following:

| What did it | sound
look
feel
taste
smell | like? |

| How did it | sound?
look?
feel?
taste?
smell? |

| It | sounded
looked
felt
tasted
smelt | interesting
modern
strange
delicious
rotten |

| It | sounded like Bach
looked like sand
felt like silk
tasted like gin
smelt like arsenic |

2.6.2 Asking about an event

> Text: John opened the door
> Question: 1) Who opened the door?
> 2) What did John open?
> 3) What did John **do**?
> 4) What **happened**?

In questions 3 and 4, less information is available to the question asker. Questions making use of **happen** are very useful since they produce complete sentences in a wholly natural way. Perhaps they should be taught at an early stage:

> Ben is buying a book.—What is happening in picture 1?
> The boys play football on Monday.—What happens on Monday?

2.6.3 Asking for reasons, purposes

> Why are they waiting at the lights?
> What are they waiting at the lights **for**?

NB: a) **What ... for is** extremely common in asking about purpose. Perhaps it is under-used in the classroom.

b) **For** must occupy final position, otherwise the meaning changes:

> For what are they singing?—For money
> What are they singing for?—Because they like it

c) **Why** and **what ... for** are frequently interchangeable, but not always. **Why ... not** cannot be replaced by **what ... not ... for**:

> He can't come because he's ill
> ⇐ Why can't he come?

d) Notice the possible answers to a why/what ... for question:

He left early	**because**	he was bored
	in case	he missed the bus
	in order to	catch his bus
	so that	he could walk home
	to	get away from Tim
	so as (not) to	have time to think

2.6.4 Asking for evidence

> Teacher: Is John tired?   Teacher: How do you know?
> Pupil: Yes   How can you tell?
>   Why do you think so?

2.7 MISCELLANEOUS SAMPLE QUESTIONS

2.7.1 Date

What is the date today?
What date is it today?
What's today's date?
What day is it?
What month is it?
What year is it?
What's the date next Thursday?
What was the date last Wednesday?
What day is the 15th?
Is the 19th a Friday or a Saturday?
What month follows/comes after June?
What is the day before Tuesday called?

2.7.2 Time

What time is it?
What's the time?
What time do you make it?
Have you got the right time?
Do you have a watch?
Note: **What time do you make it?** is colloquial and frequent. Suitable replies
might be:

> **I make it** ten to seven
> **I make the time** five past two

See also Unit 3, section B1.

2.7.3 Weather

What is the weather like?
Is it cold or hot?
What is the forecast for next week?
What temperature is it?
Is it below freezing?
How many degrees below is it?
Do you think it will snow/thaw?
What season is it?
Is it raining/snowing/sleeting/hailing/thundering?

Notice: **It's 25 below zero, It's plus 10 in the sun** as possible replies to questions
about temperature.

2.7.4 Identity

Who are you?
What is your name? How do you spell it?
What is your English name?
Where do you live?
What is your address?
Which part of —land are you from?
Where are you from?
Where do you come from?
Whereabouts is that?
Whereabouts in Tokyo do you live?
How old are you?
Have you any brothers or sisters?
What are their names?
Which school do you go to?
Whose class are you in?
Who is your class teacher?
Who is your English teacher?

2.7.5 Interests and hobbies

What are you interested in?
Have you got any hobbies?
What do you do in your spare time?
Do you play ice-hockey/baseball/football/basketball/volleyball?
Do you do a lot of reading?
Do you watch a lot of TV?
Do you go to the cinema a lot?
What do you do at weekends?
How do you spend your evenings?
Are you in any clubs?
Are you a member of any clubs?
What do you usually do on Fridays?
Have you ever been to Sweden?
Where did you spend your summer holidays?
What did you get for Christmas?
What do you hope to become?
Have you any plans for the summer/the future?

There is, of course, no limit to these questions. Their use will depend on the level of the learners. Notice, however, that they may be real questions—if the teacher does not know the answer—and that they take place in a pseudo-social situation.

Notice: Not: ★ Have you ever been *in* Sweden?
 but: **Have you ever been to Sweden?**

2.7.6 Opinion

What did you think of it?
How did you like it?
How did you find it?
Did you think it was worth going?
What was your impression of it?
What was your opinion of the film?

Was it to your liking?
Did you enjoy it?
Did you find it boring?
Which parts did you like most?
Was there anything you didn't like about the story?

Notice the replies:

I	considered found thought	it	very	enjoyable interesting boring

See also Unit 10, section P9.

2.7.7 Preference

Which did you like better?
Did you prefer this to the last chapter?
Did you like this more/better than last time?
If you had to choose, which would you take?
Which did you enjoy most of all?
Which of the three did you prefer most?
Would you rather go to Britain (or stay at home)?
Would you rather read than listen to music?
Who is your favourite actor/poet/singer?

2 EXERCISES

I. 'Yes–No' Questions

Use the following sentence frames to produce negative questions, as in the example.

> You/live in London (DO)?
> Don't you live in London?

Refer back to 2.2.2 in case of difficulty.

1. The answer/at the back of the book (BE)?
2. You/find the right page (CAN)?
3. You/get the last question right (DID)?
4. It/a good idea to look the word up in a dictionary (WOULD BE)?
5. You/come out and write the answer on the board (WILL)?
6. You/very interested in the energy crisis (BE)?
7. We/type out what we've written (COULD)?
8. It/help if we switched the lights off (MIGHT)?
9. You/finish off your essays by Friday's lesson (WILL HAVE)?
10. You/have enough time to do it before the bell went (HAD)?

II. 'Or' Questions

> 1. Did John or Bill score the goal?
> 2. Did John score the goal or (did) Bill?
> 3. Did John score the goal or did Bill score it?
> 4. Who scored the goal, John or Bill?

Ask 'Or' questions about the following sentences. Use the alternatives given in brackets and the form indicated by the numbers above.

1. He gets up at 10 o'clock on Sundays. (11 o'clock) (1; 4)
2. Mr Watt is painting the table. (Mr Lane) (2; 3)
3. He washes the car on Saturday afternoons. (go for a walk) (1; 2)
4. Susan likes Bill's dog better. (mine) (1; 4)
5. The children left for Paris on Friday evening. (London) (2; 3)
6. Charles Dickens completed 'Great Expectations' in 1861. (1862) (3; 4)

III. WH-Questions

NB: The following exercise is not meant to provide a model of the type of questions teachers should ask when dealing with a text. It merely revises some of the main difficulties.

Write WH-questions to fit the words in **bold type** in the following sentences. If the sentence is marked (tell), the question should begin **Can anyone tell me** . . .
If the sentence is marked (think), you should insert . . . **do you think** . . . in the question.

Example:

> Mary is **19**.   —How old is Mary?
> Mary is **19**. (tell)   —Can anyone tell me how old Mary is?
> Mary is **19**. (think) —How old do you think Mary is?

1. **Guiseppe's** class is going to arrange some interviews.

   _____

2. The tourists **also** visited the **British** Museum.

   _____

3. Mr. Johnson is intending to buy a **Morris Ital**. (tell)

   _____

4. The eager shopper was looking for a **red** nylon pullover.

   _____

5. The piece of apple pie she gave me tasted **absolutely delicious**. (think)

   _____

6. The village is **five kilometres** away.

   _____

7. There wasn't enough **food** in the trees.

   _____

8. **Nothing at all** happened when the bandit pulled the trigger. (think)

   _____

9. The Finnish for 'thankyou' is **Kiitos**. (tell)

   _____

10. Computers can **also** be used **for controlling traffic**.

    _____

11. After the traffic lights the red van turned **right**. (tell)

    _____

12. John was looking forward to a quiet evening **with my sister**. (think)

    _____

13. They spend **two hours** a day practising their skating.

    _____

    _____

2 EXERCISES

14. The house they want to buy is **warm and comfortable.**

_____

15. ˷The American tourists left for Edinburgh on the **16.25** train.

_____

_____

16. The lady bought **her daughter** three red balloons, too.

_____

_____

17. He takes **a size 44** shoe. (tell)

_____

18. The name of the book John forgot to bring was **'Target'**. (think)

_____

_____

19. The 29th is a **Tuesday**.

_____

20. The doctor realized that there were no **pills** left.

_____

21. The victorious colonel was seen leaving with **Miss Taylor**.

_____

22. She has had to put up with a lot of criticism from **Jack**. (think)

_____

_____

23. Marilyn was looking for a **55-year-old** millionaire.

_____

_____

24. The naughty girl stole a little piece of **the bilberry pie**. (think)

_____

_____

25. She was hoping to find time to write a short letter **to her sister**.

_____

_____

26. Modern children seem to have too much **money**.

_____

27. Ben bought the box of chocolates **for his grandmother**. (tell)

_____

_____

28. The girl started crying **because she was disappointed**.

29. **Twenty-five** of the boys took part in the competition (tell)

30. Mr Brown will be in London **for three days**. (think)

IV.
Work in groups of four. Choose any short reading text, say 25–40 lines in length. Everybody reads it through once and then turns it over. Now take it in turns to improvise five comprehension questions on the text. The person asking should not look at the text either. Ideally, there should be three WH-questions, one Yes–No question and one 'Or' question. Score one point for each question asked which the others cannot answer, but which you yourself can answer.

V.
Work in pairs. Re-read the questions listed in sections 2.7.4 and 2.7.5. Each person has two minutes to try to ask as many of the questions as possible and to try to remember the answers. At the end of the two minutes, the other person can check how much has been remembered by asking the same questions.

ANSWERS

I

1. Isn't it at the back of the book?
2. Can't you find the right page?
3. Didn't you get the last question right?
4. Wouldn't it be a good idea to look the word up in a dictionary?
5. Won't you come out and write the answer on the board?
6. Aren't you very interested in the energy crisis?
7. Couldn't you type out what you've written?
8. Mightn't it help if you switched the lights off?
9. Won't you have finished your essay by Friday?
10. Hadn't you had enough time to finish it off before the bell rang?

II

1. Does he get up at 10 o'clock or 11 o'clock on Sundays?
    What time does he get up on Sundays, 10 o'clock or 11 o'clock?
2. Is Mr Watt painting the table or (is) Mr Lane?
    Is Mr Watt painting the table or is Mr Lane painting it?
3. Does he wash the car or go for a walk on Saturday afternoons?
    Does he wash the car on Saturday afternoons or go for a walk?
4. Does Susan like Bill's dog or mine better?
    Whose dog does Susan like better, Bill's or mine?

5. Did the children leave for Paris on Friday evening or London?
   Did the children leave for Paris on Friday evening or did they leave for London?
6. Did Charles Dickens complete 'Great Expectations' in 1861 or did he complete it in 1862?
   Which year did Charles Dickens complete 'Great Expectations', 1861 or 1862?

III

1. Whose class is going to arrange some interviews?
2. Which other museum did the tourists visit?/What/Where else did the tourists visit?
3. Can anyone tell me what make of car Mr Johnson is intending to buy?
4. What colour nylon pullover was the eager shopper looking for?
5. What do you think the piece of apple pie she gave me tasted like?
6. How far (away) is the village?/How far is it to the village?
7. What wasn't there enough of in the trees?
8. What do you think happened when the bandit pulled the trigger?
9. Can anyone tell me what the Finnish for 'thank you' is?
10. What else can computers be used for?

11. Can anyone tell me which way the red van turned after the traffic lights?
12. Who do you think John was looking forward to a quiet evening with?
13. How many hours a day do they spend practising their skating?
14. What is the house they want to buy like?
15. What (time) train did the American tourists leave for Edinburgh on?
16. Who else did the lady buy three red balloons (for)?
17. Can anyone tell me what size shoe he takes?
18. What do you think the name of the book John forgot to bring was?
19. What day is the 29th?
20. What did the doctor realize there were none left of?

21. Who was the victorious colonel seen leaving with?
22. Who do you think she has had to put up with a lot of criticism from?
23. How old a/What age millionaire was Marilyn looking for?
24. What do you think the naughty girl stole a little piece of?
25. Who was she hoping to find time to write a short letter to?
26. What do modern children seem to have too much of?
27. Can anyone tell me who Ben bought the box of chocolates for?
28. What did the girl start crying for? Why did the girl start crying?
29. Can anyone tell me how many of the boys took part in the competition?
30. How long do you think will Mr Brown be in London (for)?

Unit 3

A Beginning of Lesson
1 In the Corridor
2 Greetings
3 Transition to Work
4 Absences
5 Lateness
Exercises
Answers

'Are you the wise guy who's been enquiring for a classroom?'

1 • Check the following simple clothing vocabulary:

a coat	a cap	(a pair of)	gloves
an overcoat	a hat		boots
a raincoat	a fur hat		ski-boots
an anorak	a scarf		

Also notice the following:

a mac(kintosh)
a beret ['berei]
a bobble hat
(a pair of) | mittens
          | wellingtons
          | pumps
          | gym-shoes ['dʒimʃuːz]
a satchel ['sætʃl]
a briefcase

1 **Take off your things**
Take your coat(s) off
Off with your coats/things now
Put your boots over there/by the desk
Leave your boots in the corridor
Leave your gym-shoes outside (in the corridor)

2 **Hang up your things**
Hang up your coat on your peg
Hang your coat on your hook

3 **Hurry up!**
Come on (now)
Let's get started
Let's go in
Get a move on!
Step on it!
Hurry up so that I can start the lesson

4 **Come in and sit down**
Come in and close the door
Don't slam/bang the door like that
Close it like this instead

3 A BEGINNING OF LESSON

1 ● Teach reply: Good morning/afternoon, Mr/Mrs/Miss Smith/teacher.

  ● Low rising intonation indicates friendliness.

  ● 'Afternoon'. Notice the accentuation: [ˌaːftəˈnuːn].

  ★ *Good day* is wrong in the classroom.

2 ● Address question 'How are you?' to one pupil at a time.

  ● Make plentiful use of the pupils' first names.

  ● If the question 'How are you?' is directed to several pupils in succession, the tonic syllable changes:
  First pupil: How are you, Bill?
  Second pupil: And how are you, Alison?

  ● Teach appropriate replies:

> (I'm) very well, thank you
> (I'm) fine, thanks
> (I'm) not too bad, thanks
> Fine, thanks. How about you?

'Oh, the new teacher's all right. He's congenial, eager to please and responsive to suggestions.'

1 **Good morning**
Good afternoon, everybody/boys and girls/children
Good morning, Bill
Hello, everyone
Hello there, Alison

2 **How are you?**
How are you today, Bill?
How are you getting on?
How's life?
How're things with you, Alison?
How're you feeling today, Bill?
Are you feeling better today, Alison?
I hope you've recovered from your cold, Bill

3 **I hope you are all feeling well**
I hope you are all feeling fit today
I hope you have all had a nice/good weekend/holiday
How about you, Bill? What did you do during . . .

4 **Let me introduce myself**
My name is Mr/Mrs/Miss Smith and I'm your new English teacher
I'll be teaching you English this year
I'm a teacher trainee and I'll be teaching you today, tomorrow and on Wednesday
I've got five lessons with you

3 A BEGINNING OF LESSON

1 • See also Unit 9, section N4/1, and Unit 8, section K1/1.

3 • Notice the English for typical school subjects:

> history
> geography [dʒi'ɔgrəfi]
> biology [bai'ɔlədʒi]
> chemistry ['kemistri]
> physics ['fiziks]
> psychology [sai'kɔlədʒi]
> mathematics (maths)
>
> domestic science
> home economics
> (handi)craft
> P.E. (physical education)
> gym [dʒim]

4 • Most British schools start their day with an assembly in the school hall. This generally lasts 10–15 minutes. Larger schools may make use of a broadcasting system with loudspeakers in each classroom.

1 **It's time to start now**
Let's start our (English) lesson now (shall we?)
Is everybody ready to start?
I hope you are all ready for your English lesson
I think we can start now
Now we can get down to (some) work
Let's get cracking

2 **I'm waiting to start**
I'm waiting for you to be quiet
We won't start until everyone is quiet
Stop talking now so that we can start
Settle down now so we can start

3 **Put your things away**
Close your desks
Close the lid of your desk
Put that book away
This is an English lesson, not a knitting lesson

4 **Let's listen to this morning's reading**
The 'At the Start of the Day' reading is about to begin
Before we start, the headmaster has some announcements to make

5 **I'll just mark the register**
Could you pass me the register, please?
I haven't filled in the register
Take the register to room 26

3 A BEGINNING OF LESSON

1 • Teach/expect appropriate replies to suit pupils' abilities:

> I don't know/I've no idea
> I haven't seen him today
> He wasn't here yesterday, either
>
> He's ill/not well
> He wasn't feeling very well, so he went home
>
> He's at the doctor's/dentist's
> He's gone for an X-ray/a medical examination/an interview
> He has probably missed the bus
>
> He has got the flu/a cold/a temperature
> He is in bed with the flu/a cold/a temperature

★ Who is *lacking*?
Who is missing/absent/away?

2 ★ *On* the last lesson.
At/in the last lesson.

• Notice the change of tonic syllable:
Where were <u>you</u> last time, Bill?
You weren't here. Where <u>were</u> you?

1 **Who is absent today?**
Who is missing?
Who isn't here?
What's the matter with Alison today?
Has anybody seen Bill today?
What's wrong with Bill today?
Has anybody any idea where Bill is today?

2 **Who was absent last time?**
Who wasn't here on Monday?
Who missed last Wednesday's lesson?
You weren't at/in the last lesson, Bill. Where were you?
Who was away last Friday?

*'I've been off sick — has there been any swing
from informal to formal teaching methods?'*

1 • Teach appropriate apologies:

> (I'm) sorry I'm late
> I've been to see the doctor
> I've been to the dentist's
> I missed my bus
> I've been helping Mr Smith

★ *For* ten minutes ago.
Ten minutes ago.

*'There's our kid playing truant again—
and he's supposed to be taking my sick
note to school!'*

1 **Why are you late?**
   Where have you been?
   We started ten minutes ago. What have you been doing?
   Did you oversleep/miss your bus?
   What do you say when you are late?

2 **I see. Well, sit down and let's get started**
   Please hurry up and sit down. We've already started
   That's all right. Sit down and we can start

3 **Try not to be late next time**
   Try to be here on time next time
   Don't let it happen again
   Let this be the last time
   That's the second time this week
   I'll have to report you if you're late again

3 EXERCISES

I. Fill in the gaps, using an appropriate word or phrase from the following list. Notice
that there will be some phrases over.

a) oversleep
b) close the lid
c) recovered
d) miss
e) the matter with

f) absent
g) corridor
h) step on it
i) a move on
j) on time

k) got down to
l) getting on
m) wrong
n) slam
o) hang up

1. Leave your boots in the ....

2. Who was ... last time?

3. Hurry up! Get ... ... !

4. Try to be here ... ... next week.

5. How are you ... ..., Jill?

6. Please don't ... the door like that!

7. Did you ... go to bed earlier?

8. What is ... ... David today?

9. ... ... your scarf on your peg.

10. Did you ... last Wednesday's lesson?

II. Fill in the missing prepositions and adverbs, wherever necessary.

1. Try to be here ... time ... next week.

2. What's wrong ... Bill today?

3. Step ... it!

4. We started ... ten minutes ago.

5. I hope you are all ready ... your lesson.

6. Hang ... your coat ... your hook.

7. You weren't ... last Tuesday's lesson, were you?

8. Get a move ...!

9. How're things ... you, Barbara?

10. What's the matter ... Alan today?

III. Fill in 'to' or 'for', wherever necessary.

1. Try ... not ... be late next time.

2. Is everybody ready ... start now?

3. Try ... be here on time next time.

4. I'm waiting ... you ... be quiet.

5. It's time ... start.

6. Don't ... let ... it ... happen again.

7. Are you ready ... your English lesson?

8. I'm waiting ... start. Bill, we're waiting ... you.

IV. The passage below is a description of the beginning of an English lesson. At the places numbered, e.g. (1), the teacher might say something appropriate in English. What does the teacher say?

It's Monday morning and the time is 9 o'clock. You go into the classroom. Most of the pupils are already in their desks but some of them are still outside in the corridor. One boy has brought a huge bag of sports equipment with him and clearly intends to take it into the classroom. You stop him and suggest a better solution (1). One girl in the front row is wearing muddy wellingtons (2), and Franco is sitting in a thick anorak even though it is almost 20 °C outside (3). You notice that two boys are still hanging about in the corridor (4). They come in but leave the door open (5). When you ask them to close it, they slam it (6). At last everybody seems to be ready. You greet the pupils (7) and then ask Luigi and Maria how they are (8 & 9). After that you announce that it really is time to start, (10) but first you have to get their attention. Franco is chatting with Monica (11); Maria's desk is open (12); and Giorgio has got his geography books open in front of him (13). You almost forget the register (14). You check who's missing (15). You notice that Giulia is away and wonder why (16). You're planning to start off the lesson with a short test, but to be fair you check who actually attended the last lesson, which was on the previous Wednesday (17). At that very same moment the door opens and Carita comes in. It is now almost ten past nine (18). Carita explains sleepily that she was so busy studying her English vocabulary that she forgot to get off the bus. This is the second time she has been late in a week, and you make it clear that you will be very angry next time (19). At last you are ready to start your lesson (20).

V. Use the lesson description in exercise IV as the basis for a role-play. Take it in turns to play the part of the teacher. See how quickly you can get your 'pupils' to settle down. Remember that the beginning of the lesson provides plenty of opportunities for using the language naturally—ask about the pupils' weekend, talk about the weather, enquire about absentees.

ANSWERS

I	II	III
1. corridor	1. on —	1. —, to
2. absent/away/missing	2. with	2. to
3. a move on	3. on	3. to
4. on time	4. —	4. for, to
5. getting on	5. for	5. to
6. slam/bang	5. up/ —, on	6. —, —, —
7. oversleep	7. in/at	7. for
8. the matter with	8. on	8. to, for
9. Hang	9. with	
10. miss	10. with	

IV Suggested answers
1. (Why don't you) leave your sports equipment in the corridor(?)
2. Take your wellingtons off and leave them outside, please.

3 ANSWERS

3. Franco, take your anorak off and hang it up on your peg/hang it over the back of your chair.
4. Hey, you two boys, hurry up. Come in and sit down.
5. Would you mind closing the door, please.
6. Don't/there's no need to slam it like that!
7. Good morning, everybody/boys and girls.
8. How are you today, Luigi?
9. And what about you, Maria? How are you getting on?
10. OK, I think it's time for us to get down to some work.
11. Hey, Franco and Monica. Stop talking now so that we can start.
12. Close the lid of your desk, would you, Maria, please.
13. Put those books away, Giorgio. This is an English lesson, not a geography lesson.
14. I almost forgot. I haven't filled in the register.
15. Who is absent/away/not here today?
16. Does anyone know what's wrong with Giulia?
17. Who was away last Wednesday?/Did anyone miss last Wednesday's lesson?
18. Why are you late, Carita? We started ten minutes ago.
19. Don't let it happen again, will you.
20. I think we can start now.

Unit 4

'That'll do for today's lesson.'

1 • Check the following everyday ways of telling the time:

> It's (a) quarter past three ⇒ It's (a) quarter past
> It's (a) quarter to two ⇒ It's (a) quarter to
> It's ten (minutes) to/past one ⇒ It's ten to/past
> It's half past ten ⇒ It's half past/it's half ten

• Notice that the word **minutes** is generally included when the time involves numbers other than 5, 10, 15, 20, 25:
I make it five past but: **I make it three minutes past.**
In such cases approximate forms are used:

> I make it **almost** ten past
> I make it **just gone** ten to

• Notice you use the future tense even in phrases like:

> We'll stop now
> We'll finish for today

3 • In checking the time from pupils (at least in intermediate classes) note the phrase **What time do you make it**?

• Notice the following pattern:

It's not worth There's no point (in) There's no use (in) It's no use It's a waste of time	starting anything else

5 ★ I *think we haven't* got time.
I don't think we have got time.
Notice the English preference for saying 'I don't think':

> I don't think there is anything else in this lesson
> I don't think you've had this word before

1 **It's ten to ten. We'll have to stop now**
It's almost time to stop
I'm afraid it's time to finish now
I make it almost time. We'll have to stop here
I make it just gone five past. We'll have to finish there
There's the buzzer/bell, so we must stop working now
That's the buzzer/bell. It's time to stop
All right! That's all for today, thank you
Right. You can put your things away and go
That will do for today. You can go now

2 **It isn't time to finish yet**
The buzzer/bell hasn't gone yet
There are still two minutes to go
We still have a couple of minutes left
I only make it a quarter to. There's another five minutes yet
This lesson isn't supposed to/due to finish until five past
Your watch must be fast

3 **We have five minutes over**
We seem to have finished a few minutes early
My watch must be slow. I make it only a quarter to
We have an extra five minutes
It seems we have two or three minutes in hand/to spare
There isn't any point (in) starting a new exercise
There's no point (in) beginning anything else this time
Sit quietly until the bell goes
Carry on with the exercise for the rest of the lesson

4 **Wait a minute**
Hang on a moment
Just hold on a minute
Stay where you are for a moment
Just a moment, please
One more thing before you go
Don't go rushing off. I have something to tell/say to you
Back to your places!

5 **We'll finish this next time**
I don't think we've got time to finish this now
We'll do/read/look at the rest of this chapter on Thursday
We'll finish off this exercise in the next lesson
We've run out of time, but we'll go on with this exercise next time
We'll continue (with) this chapter next Monday
We'll continue working on this chapter next time

- Notice the following additional phrases:

> Please re-read this chapter for Friday's lesson
> Revise what we did today and then try exercise 4
> Go through this section again on your own at home
> This was your homework from last time
> You were supposed to do this exercise for homework

★ *The* exercise 10 on *the* page 23.
No articles!

★ *Until* page 175.
Down to/as far as page 175.

★ The *two last* chapters.
Notice the word order with 'first, last, next'!
The last two chapters.

2 • Paragraph = one part of a reading passage.
Chapter = a lesson with a number or title.
Notice also the increasingly common words *unit* and *module*.

★ Will you *do this to the end* at home.
Will you finish this (off) at home.

- Notice the phrases:

> Which question are you on?
> How far have you got?
> Where are you up to?

3 ★ *On* the next lesson.
In the next lesson.

1 **This is your homework**
This chapter/lesson/page/exercise is your homework
This is your homework for tonight/today/next time
For your homework would you do exercise 10 on page 23
Prepare the last two chapters for Monday
Prepare as far as/down to/up to page 175
Your homework for tonight is to prepare chapter 17
I'm not going to set (you) any homework this time

2 **Finish this off at home**
Finish off the exercise at home
Do the rest of the exercise as your homework for tonight
You will have to/must read the last paragraph at home
Complete this exercise at home
Finish the question you're (working) on at the moment, and do the rest at home

3 **There will be a test on this next Wednesday**
I shall give you a test on these lessons/chapters sometime next week
Learn the vocabulary because I shall be giving you a test on it in the next lesson
You can expect a test on this in the near future
Please revise lessons 9 and 10. There will be a test on them sometime

4 **Don't forget about your homework!**
Remember your homework
Please pick up a copy of the exercise as you leave
Remember to take a sheet as you leave
Collect a copy of your homework from my desk

1 • Low rising intonation indicates friendliness and cheerfulness.

   • Teach appropriate replies: as teacher's phrases.

2 • In normal everyday speech years are read as two separate numbers:

> 1977 = nineteen seventy-seven
> 1950 = nineteen fifty
> 1902 = | nineteen two
> | nineteen o two
> 1900 = nineteen hundred

3 • Low-rising intonation.

   • Possible reply to 'Don't work too hard':
     'Don't worry, we won't.'

   • **Weekend.** Notice the accentuation: [wi:kˈend].

'*It's my day off . . .*'

1   **Goodbye**
Goodbye, boys and girls
Bye-bye, children
G'bye, everyone
Cheerio, Bill
Bye now, Alison

2   **See you again on Tuesday**
I'll see you (all) again next Wednesday
See you tomorrow afternoon again
I'll be seeing some of you again after the break
I'll see you all again after Christmas/next year/in 1982

3   **Have a nice weekend**
Have a good holiday/Christmas/Easter
Enjoy your holiday
Don't work too hard
I hope you all have a nice vacation

4   **Tomorrow we'll meet in room 14**
I'll see you in room 7 after the break
Wait outside the language laboratory for me
There's been a change of room for next week
We'll be meeting in room 19 instead
Which period do we have English on Friday?
The 4th period has been cancelled next Tuesday so there won't be an English lesson

5   **I won't be here next week**
Miss Jones will take/be taking you instead
Go and join class 6B for your English lesson
I'll leave him/her some work to give you
This was my last lesson with you

1 • Notice the idiomatic word order in the following:

> Up you get!
> Off you go!
> Out you go!

'Remember the trouble we used to have getting them out?'

3 • In beginners' classes, the following game can be used effectively when dismissing the pupils. The teacher (or a pupil) points to pupils in turn, saying the rhyme:

> One, two, three,
> Out goes he/she

The choice of 'he' or 'she' is made according to the sex of the last pupil pointed to. The cycle continues until only one pupil remains.

Other rhyme variations include:

> One, two, three, four
> Out goes one more
>
> One and two
> Out go you

1 **Will you please go out**
Everybody outside!
All of you, get outside now!
Hurry up and get out!

2 **Go out quietly**
Not so much noise, please
Quietly!
Ssshhh!
Try not to make any noise as you leave
No noise as you leave. Other classes are still working

3 **Queue up by the door**
Get into a queue
Form/make a queue and wait until the buzzer goes
Go and join the back of the queue

4 **Wash your hands before you go**
Come and wash your hands before your lunch
Have you all washed your hands?

5 **Open the window**
Let's have some fresh air
It's very stuffy in here
Let in some fresh air for the next class

4 EXERCISES

I. Fill in the gaps, using an appropriate word or phrase from the following list.

a) break
b) gone
c) revise
d) will do
e) carry on
f) due to
g) hang on

h) rest
i) finish off
j) point in
k) rushing off
l) in hand
m) make
n) chapter

o) queue up
p) paragraph
q) down
r) bell
s) as far as
t) set
u) fast

1. Thank you. That ... ... for today.

2. All right, there isn't any ... ... starting exercise 5.

3. Look at page 72, the third ... from the top.

4. Don't go ... . Wait a moment.

5. Please ... ... by the door and wait.

6. Please ... ... exercise 11A at home.

7. Please prepare ... 27 for next time.

8. I'll be seeing some of you again after the ....

9. Well, we seem to have a few minutes ... .

10. There's the .... We shall have to stop here.

11. Don't move! This lesson isn't ... ... to finish until ten.

12. ... a moment. I have something to say to you.

13. Prepare this passage ... the bottom of page 16.

14. Ssshhh! The bell hasn't ... yet.

15. I make it ten to. My watch must be ....

II. Rewrite the following sentences, using the more English form 'I don't think . . .'

1. I think we didn't finish this exercise off last time.
2. I think this word isn't very common.
3. I think you haven't really understood my question.
4. I think you won't need this phrase very often.
5. I think you don't know this word.
6. I think there are no problems in this sentence.
7. I think nobody has prepared this chapter, have they?
8. I think you will never need this phrase.
9. I think there is nothing else to say about this chapter, is there?
10. I think none of you made any really bad mistakes.
11. I think we haven't had this word before.
12. I think you will see this phrase nowhere else in the book.

III. Fill in the missing prepositions and adverbs.

1. That's all ... today.

2. We have run ... ... time, but you can finish it ... at home.

3. Please hold ... for a minute.

4. We'll go ... this exercise next time.

5. Complete the question you're ... at the moment.

6. I want you to prepare chapter 25, ... line 27.

7. There will be a test ... these chapters next Wednesday.

8. Please complete this work ... next Friday's lesson.

9. ... your homework, please learn the vocabulary.

10. Where are you ... ..., Bill? Have you finished the exercise?

11. Translate this passage into English, ... line 13.

12. This is your homework ... today.

13. Would you finish exercise 13A ... page 56, please.

14. OK, sit quietly ... the rest of the lesson.

15. All right, boys. Get ... a queue by the door.

IV. Practise telling the time, using the phrase 'I make it . . .' and the approximations 'almost' and 'just gone', where appropriate. The time given in brackets is when the lesson is due to finish. Think of some suitable comment.

Example: 9.51 (9.55)
I make it just gone ten to ten, and this lesson isn't due to finish until five to, so carry on with the exercise until the bell goes.

1. 12.02 (12.10)	5. 14.59 (15.00)
2. 10.29 (10.25)	6. 10.00 (10.10)
3. 11.30 (11.30)	7. 11.06 (11.00)
4. 09.46 (09.50)	8. 12.31 (12.35)

V. The following conversation takes place at the end of an English lesson. By looking at what the pupils say, it is possible to fill in the part of the teacher.

Teacher:	(1)
Nicos:	I don't know. I haven't got a watch.
Teacher:	(2)
Vassos:	Almost ten to.
Teacher:	(3)
Vassos:	Well, I'm only putting my things away in my desk.
Teacher:	(4)

Nicos:	But Vassos makes it ten to now!
Teacher:	(5)
Nicos:	At last! I thought it would never go.
Teacher:	(6)
Vassos:	It certainly will do! What a terrible lesson!
Teacher:	(7)
Nicos:	Oh no, not the same exercise again!
Teacher:	(8)
Alexandra:	I wasn't rushing off anywhere. OK, what do you want to say?
Teacher:	(9)
Alexandra:	I missed that. What chapter was it we're supposed to prepare?
Helene:	Seven, down to line 32, for next Monday.
Teacher:	(10)
Helene:	Oh no, not a vocabulary test as well!
Teacher:	(11)
Nicos:	You won't see me at least. I've got to go to the dentist's on Monday.
Teacher:	(12)
Vassos:	What sort of weekend is that when you've got to revise for a vocabulary test?
Teacher:	(13)
Nicos:	All right, we're going, don't worry.
Teacher:	(14)
Nicos:	We can be quiet if we want. After all, the others need some quiet as well.
Teacher:	(15)
Vassos:	I'll open it for you.
Teacher:	(16)
Vassos:	Yes, cheerio.

VI. Role-play the conversation in exercise V, but imagine that:

A) 1. it's the last lesson before the Christmas holiday.
   2. the homework is to finish off the exercise started in class.
   3. the pupils have their school dinner after your lesson.

B) 1. your lesson has been moved to room 11 next week.
   2. you don't intend to set any homework.
   3. your lesson finishes ten minutes before other classes finish.

C) 1. you are going to be away next week.
   2. the homework is unit 10, exercises A and B.
   3. you won't be seeing the pupils again until after the summer vacation.

ANSWERS

I

1. will do	9. in hand
2. point in	10. bell
3. paragraph	11. due to
4. rushing off	12. hang on
5. queue up	13. as far as
6. finish off	14. gone
7. chapter	15. fast
8. break	

II

1. I don't think we finished this exercise last time.
2. I don't think this word is very common.
3. I don't think you have really understood my question.
4. I don't think you will need this phrase very often.
5. I don't think you know this word.
6. I don't think there are any problems in this sentence.
7. I don't think anybody has prepared this chapter, have they?
8. I don't think you will ever need this phrase.
9. I don't think there is anything else to say about this chapter, is there?
10. I don't think any of you made any really bad mistakes.
11. I don't think we've had this word before.
12. I don't think you will see this phrase anywhere else in the book.

III

1. for	9. For
2. out of, off	10. up to
3. on	11. as far as
4. on with	12. for
5. on	13. on
6. down to/up to	14. for
7. on	15. into
8. for	

IV Suggested answers

1. . . . there's another seven or eight minutes yet.
2. . . . my watch must be fast.
3. Aah, there's the bell. It's time to stop.
4. It seems we have three or four minutes in hand.
5. The bell will be going any minute now.
6. Carry on with the exercise for the rest of the lesson.
7. The bell should have gone six minutes ago.
8. There isn't any point in starting a new exercise, so you can just sit quietly until the bell goes.

V Suggested answers

1. What time do you make it, Nicos?
2. What time do *you* make it, then, Vassos?
3. It isn't time to finish yet, Vassos.
4. The lesson isn't due to finish until ten to.
5. There's the bell. We'll have to stop here.
6. That will do for today.
7. We'll go on with this exercise next time.
8. Don't go rushing off, Alexandra. I have something to say to you.
9. For your homework prepare chapter seven down to line 32 for next Monday.
10. You'd better revise your vocabulary because there will be a test on it.
11. Well, I'll see you all again on Monday.
12. All right, have a nice weekend, everybody.
13. Now hurry up and get out, please.
14. And not so much noise. Other classes are still working.
15. It's rather stuffy in here. Could someone open the window.
16. Thank you, Vassos. Bye-bye.

Unit 5

C Set Phrases

1 Seasonal, Occasional
2 Apologies
3 Thanking, Giving
4 Warnings
Exercises
Answers

'She never misses.'

1 • Although there are no name-days in Britain, you could still say: **Happy name-day, Lisa,** or **Today (it) is Lisa's name-day.**

2 • Teach appropriate replies:

> Thank you, the same to you
> Thanks, same to you

★ It is incorrect to reply: Thank you, *the same* (for you).

★ *Merry* Easter; *Merry* New Year.
Happy Easter/New Year.

Merry Christmas can be considered the exception.
• Notice also: *April/All Fools' Day* (1st April) and *Bonfire/Guy Fawkes' Night* (5th November).
April Fool!—used of someone who has been caught out on April 1st.

3 • Used when someone sneezes.

★ Catching *a* flu.
Catching the flu.

4 • Might be used before an important examination or a sports event involving pupils in the class.

• Possible replies:

> Thank you/Thanks, I'll/we'll need it

5 • The teacher might ask:

> How did you get on with your test?
> How did the game go last week?
> How did you get on on Sunday?

6 • **Congratulations** may also be used for an engagement.

7 • [ʌpsəˈdeizi] Used when you stumble or nearly drop something.

• Notice other vocalizations: [wou] = slow down, stop; [ʃuː] = go away; [autʃ] = that hurts.

1 **Happy birthday!**
   Many happy returns (of the day), Bill
   Bill has his/a birthday today
   Alison is eleven today. Let's sing 'Happy Birthday'

2 **Merry Christmas!**
   I hope you all have a good Christmas
   Happy New Year!
   All the best for the New Year
   Happy Easter

3 **God bless!**
   Bless you!/God bless you!
   I hope you're not catching/getting a cold
   It sounds as though you're getting the flu

4 **Good luck!**
   Best of luck
   I hope you win/get through/pass

5 **Hard luck!**
   Hard lines!
   Never mind!
   Better luck next time!

6 **Well done!**
   Congratulations

7 **Oops-a-daisy!**
   Oops!

8 **Remember me to your brother**
   Give my regards/best wishes to your sister
   Say hello to your sister for me

5 C SET PHRASES

1 • Low rising intonation.

   • Teach appropriate replies:

   > That's all right
   > It doesn't matter
   > No, it was <u>my</u> fault

2 • Pupils may initiate a similar conversation:

   > Could I leave ten minutes before the end?
   > Is it all right if I leave at twenty to?

3 • Less polite forms include: **Shift! Budge! Move!**

   • **Excuse me:** used for passing people, moving in front of their line of vision, reaching across in front of them, interrupting their conversation.

   ★ You are *on* my way.
   In my way.

   • For your case = **because of** your case.

4 • I'm feeling a bit **under the weather** = I'm not very well.

1 **Sorry**
I'm very/terribly/awfully sorry (about that)
Sorry about that
Sorry, that was my fault
I *am* sorry

2 **Excuse me for a moment**
I'll be back in a moment
Carry on with that exercise while I'm away
Would you excuse me for a while/moment
I've just got to go next door for a moment

3 **Excuse me**
Mind out of the way
Mind out!
Could I get past, please
Out of the way now!
Get out of my/the way
You're in the/my way
You're blocking the gangway
Bill can't get past for your case

4 **I'm afraid I'm not feeling very well today**
I'm afraid I can't speak any louder
I seem to be losing my voice
I have a sore throat
I have (a bit of) a headache
I'm feeling a bit under the weather
Do you mind if I sit down?
If you don't mind, I'll sit

5 **I've made a mistake on the board**
I'm sorry, I didn't notice it
I must have overlooked it
I must be getting absent-minded in my old age

5 C SET PHRASES

1 • Teach appropriate replies:

> That's all right
> Not at all
> Don't mention it
> Think nothing of it
> Any time

2 • These phrases accompany the action of giving.

★ Do not say *please* when you give something!

• Encourage the use of these phrases when distributing name-cards, exercises, tests, etc.

'*I passed your house yesterday evening.*'
'*Thanks.*'

1 **Thank you**
   Thank you very much
   Thanks a lot
   Thanks for your help
   Thank you for cleaning the blackboard
   It was very kind of you to help. Thank you
   I really do appreciate your help

2 **Here you are**
   There you are
   This is for you, Alison
   And here's one for you, Bill
   Take it. It's for you
   Help yourself (to a copy)

'*M..A..R..Y!... Someone wants to listen to you.*'

5 C SET PHRASES

1 ● **Duck** means 'lower your head!' **Mind out** means 'get out of the way'. **Look out** and **watch out** = 'be careful' or 'it's dangerous!'

● Note the various uses of the word **mind**:

> If you don't **mind**, I'll stop you there
> Do you **mind** if I stop you there?
> Would you **mind** repeating that?
> **Mind** the cable!
> **Mind** you don't slip!
> Never **mind** about the tense
> You haven't got a book? Well, never **mind**

2 ● Notice the patterns:

Mind Be careful Careful Watch	you don't	bang your head on the door drop the tape recorder spill that paint knock the projector over

Mind Be careful of/with Careful of/with Watch Watch out for	the projector the screen the cable that window the lead [li:d]

3 ● Threats will probably be given in the native language. The English equivalents of some possible deterrents are:

> You will be in detention next week
> You can stay behind after school next week
> I'll send you to see the headmaster
> You can go and stand outside for a while
> Come and see me after the lesson
> I want to see you outside the teachers' room at 11

1   **Look out!**
Watch out!
Mind!
Mind out!
Duck!

2   **Be careful!**
Be careful you don't drop that
Mind you don't hurt your head
Mind the step
Watch you don't trip over the cable
Watch your step

3   **Stop doing that, or else!**
Be quiet or else you can go and sit on your own
If you don't be quiet, I'll send you out
One more word and you can stay behind after school
This is the last time I'm warning you
Look! I've just about had enough from you
I won't tell you again. Next time it's the headmaster for you
Don't push your luck with me
You're heading the right way for trouble
Once more and you've had it

5 EXERCISES

I. Fill in the gaps:

a) get on	i) help yourself
b) bless you	j) trip over
c) look	k) get past
d) mind out	l) gangway
e) blocking	m) excuse
f) remember	n) same to you
g) returns	o) losing
h) under	p) on with

1. Many happy ... of the day, Pauline!

2. ... ...! I can't get past for your big feet.

3. I want you to carry ... this exercise while I'm away.

4. I seem to be ... my voice.

5. I'm feeling a bit ... the weather. I think I need a holiday.

6. ... ...! I hope you're not catching a cold.

7. Mind you don't ... ... Bill's bag.

8. ... out! You're going to knock the screen over!

9. Please ... me for a moment. I have to fetch something.

10. Your sister was in my class five years ago. Please ... me to her.

11. How did you ... ... in the chess competition last week?

12. Your bag is ... the .... Please move it.

II. Translate this teacher's thoughts into words, using the word 'mind' in some way each time.

1. 'Look at this fool, standing right in my way.'
2. 'He's not looking what he's doing and the tape-recorder is right behind him.'
3. 'She's a tall girl. She's going to hit her head on the door.'
4. 'Why has she got such a soft voice? I can never hear what she says.'
5. 'He'll make a mistake with the tense anyway, so why worry about it.'
6. 'That's the second time this week she's knocked the water over, but I don't suppose it's worth making a fuss about it.'
7. 'I've got a terrible headache. I think I'd feel better if I sat down.'
8. 'None of them have any idea about punctuation, so there's no point in taking marks off for mistakes.'

III. The passage below is a description of an English lesson. At the places numbered, e.g. (1), the teacher might say something appropriate in English. What does the teacher say?

It's the last English lesson before the Christmas holidays. At the beginning of the lesson you apologize—you still haven't recovered from a stomach upset and aren't feeling too well (1). You are hoping that you won't have to shout as there seems to be something wrong with your voice (2). Inge sneezes (3). A lot of the pupils have been away recently with colds, and Peter appears to be catching one, too, because he sneezes (4). Some of the boys in the class play in the school basketball team and the previous Friday they had a game against a local school (5). Unfortunately, they were just beaten 87–88 (6). But Hans scored 25 points and won the prize for the best player (7). It also happens to be his birthday today (8). As it is the last lesson, you have decided to show a film. You walk to the back of the class to plug in the projector. On the way you accidentally tread on Karl-Heinz's toes (9). The lead for the projector is too short so you have to go to the neighbouring classroom to fetch an extension (10). When you return you find Ilona sitting in the gangway, which makes it very difficult for you to get past (11). Renate—a very helpful pupil—has already drawn the curtains (12). Brigitte tries to help, too, but almost succeeds in knocking over the projector (13). Klaus rushes to turn the lights off, and has to be warned about the lead on the floor (14). Dieter, who has the reputation of being the clumsiest boy, fetches the film from your desk. You have to remind him to be careful (15). When he actually succeeds in bringing it to you in one piece, you congratulate him rather ironically (16).

The film itself is a disappointment and it isn't long before the pupils start chatting amongst themselves. You warn them several times and finally threaten them—they won't enjoy an extra hour at school on the last day (17). Eberhard is reading a comic, so you reach across in front of Eva (18) to warn him. One of the pupils accidentally pulls the plug out of the wall and apologizes. You assure her it isn't important (19). When the film finally finishes, you give them appropriate wishes for the time of year (20).

IV. Clear an empty space in the middle of the classroom. Then place some obstacles in the space (e.g. chairs, books, cases). Three people are blindfolded and must move around in the empty space without bumping into the obstacles or each other. The others shout warnings.

V. Start lessons which include some of the following features:
A) — it's near Christmas
   — one of the pupils sneezes
   — one of the pupils has failed her driving test
   — you missed a mistake on the blackboard

B) — it's near Easter
   — one of the pupils has a 12th birthday
   — you accidentally bump into one of the pupils
   — you have a sore throat

C) — you are having a lot of trouble with one pupil
   — one of the pupils has given you a lot of help with your class English newspaper
   — you notice a mistake you have made on the board
   — you know the brother of one of the pupils

5 ANSWERS

I.

1. returns	7. trip over
2. mind out	8. look
3. on with	9. excuse
4. losing	10. remember
5. under	11. get on
6. Bless you!	12. blocking, gangway

II

1. Mind out of the way!
2. Mind the tape recorder!
3. Mind you don't bang your head!/Mind your head!
4. Would/Do you mind repeating what you said?
5. Never mind about the tense.
6. Never mind.
7. If you don't mind, I'll sit down.
8. I don't mind about punctuation mistakes.

III Suggested answers

1. I'm afraid I'm not feeling very well today.
2. I'm afraid I seem to be losing my voice so I won't be able to speak any louder.
3. Bless you, Inge!
4. God bless, Peter! It sounds as though you're catching a cold.
5. How did the game go on Friday?
6. Hard luck!/Never mind!
7. Well done, Hans.
8. Many happy returns of the day, Hans.
9. I'm awfully sorry.
10. Excuse me for a moment. I've just got to go next door.
11. Mind out of the way, Ilona. You're blocking the gangway and I can't get past.
12. Thank you for drawing the curtains, Renate. It was very kind of you to help.
13. Watch out! You're going to knock the projector over if you're not careful.
14. Be careful you don't trip over the lead, Klaus.
15. Please be very careful with the film, Dieter.
16. Congratulations, Dieter.
17. If you don't be quiet, you can stay behind for an hour after school today.
18. Excuse me, please, Eva.
19. It doesn't matter/Never mind.
20. Merry Christmas, everyone/I hope you all have a nice Christmas.

Unit 6

D Textbook Activity

'Last time I was in here they taught me to read and write—now I'm in for forgery.'

1 Check the following vocabulary:

Give out the Collect in the	BOOKS	PAPERS
	workbooks	sheets
	textbooks	texts
	readers	passages
	dictionaries	wordlists
		handouts
	MATERIAL	exercises
	folders	tests
	topics	questions
	subjects	question sheets
	workcards	answers
	scorecards	answer sheets
	essay titles	words of the song
	study packs	model answers
	sets of material	

'*Sorry—books are a minority interest.*'

1 **Give out the books, please**
Pass out the exercises
Pass these (to the) back
Take one and pass them on
Get the books out of the cupboard and give them out
Take the books off the shelf/out of the bookcase
Fetch the dictionaries from the teachers' room/staff room

2 **Has everybody got a book?**
Have you all got a copy of the exercise?
Is there anybody without (a book)?
Is there anybody who hasn't got a copy?
Can everybody see (a copy of) the text/passage?
Where's your book, Alison?

3 **Don't forget it next time**
Remember it (for) next time
Make sure you bring it on Friday
Be sure to remember it next Monday
Don't anybody forget their book next time

4 **One book between two**
One between two
One book to every three pupils
Three pupils to each book
There's one dictionary/set of pictures for each group

5 **You will have to share with Bill**
Could you share (with Alison), please
There are only enough for ten pupils
Share with Bill this time
I'm afraid I haven't got enough (copies) to go round
I'm afraid there aren't enough for everybody

6 D TEXTBOOK ACTIVITY

1 • Note the reduced forms:

> Hands up! = Up with your hands!
> Books out! = Out with your books!
> Books away! = Away with your books!

2 • Notice the prepositions:

> **Open** your books **at** page 56
> The exercise **is on** page 56
> I want you to **turn to** page 56

★ Take out your books and *open at* page 10.
'Open' requires an object: Take out your books and open **them** at page 10.

• Page numbers
1–99: as a full number, e.g. 32—thirty-two
100–: either as a full number (129—one hundred and twenty-nine) or, for clarity, as individual numbers (one-two-nine)

• Always remember the **and** in numbers over a hundred
167 = one hundred **and** sixty-seven

• The '0' in numbers like 107 is pronounced [ou]

4 • Check the following textbook vocabulary:

advertisement	index
article	interview
cartoon	list
checklist	map
comic strip	passage
conversation	photograph
crossword	picture
diagram	reminder
dialogue	sketch
drawing	statistics
extract	summary
figures	table
guide	wordlist
illustration	

1 **Get your books out**
   Take out your workbooks
   Books out, please!
   You'll need your workbooks
   Out with your books, please

2 **Open your books at page 27**
   Take out your books and open them at page 123/lesson 12
   Open your books, please
   You'll find the exercise on page 206
   Look at page 19
   Look at exercise 5A on page 46
   Have a look at the diagram on page 25
   It's somewhere near the front/back/middle of the book
   It's on the inside cover at the back
   The name is on the back cover/the title page

3 **Now turn to page 16**
   Turn over
   Turn over the page
   Over the page
   Turn to the next page
   Next page, please
   Let's move on to the next page
   I want you to turn on to page 134

4 **Turn back to page 16**
   Turn back to the previous page
   Now look back at the last chapter
   Keep one finger in the vocabulary list at the back
   You can refer to the map/list on page 216
   Refer back to the grammar notes on page 23
   Look across at the other side
   Use the index at the back of the book

6 D TEXTBOOK ACTIVITY

1 ● Notice the idiomatic uses of **on**:

> You have had long enough **on** this
> I want you to work **on** this in pairs
> Finish off the question you are **on**
> Last time we were **on** the subject of medicine
> We have quite a lot of work to do **on** this

2 ★ *Put* your books *upside down.*
   Turn your books over.

3 ● Notice the word order possibilities with phrasal verbs like **put away, collect in, finish off, hand in**:

Put your books away	Put away your books	Put them away
Collect the tests in	Collect in the tests	Collect them in
Finish the test off	Finish off the test	Finish it off
Hand your sheet in	Hand in your sheet	Hand it in

NB: there is only one correct position in the case of pronouns. The following are incorrect:

★ Put *away them*
★ Collect *in them*
★ Finish *off it*
★ Hand *in it*

Where the particle functions as a preposition (e.g. *through, over*) the object, whether noun or pronoun, must follow the preposition:

Let's just run through this exercise—Let's run through it
Could we just go over the details again—Go over them again

Notice that *go* and *run* are used intransitively.

4 ● Hand in your | translations | dialogues | stories
                | summaries | essays | compositions
                | dictations | test papers | projects

100

1 **Stop working now**
   Would you stop writing, please
   Pens/pencils down
   Put your pens/pencils down
   I'm afraid I'll have to stop you now
   Time is up. Stop writing
   I think you've had long enough on this
   I'm afraid it's time to stop
   Would you finish off the sentence you are on

2 **Close your books**
   All books closed, please
   Turn your books over
   Put your books face down
   Put your books away now
   I don't want to see any books open/on your desks
   Shut your books

3 **Collect the books in**
   Collect the readers in and put them away
   Pass the sheets to the front (of each row)
   Don't forget to put/write your names on them
   Could the first person in each row collect the books, please

4 **Hand in your papers as you leave**
   Leave your essays/sheets/tests on the desk as you go out
   Have you all handed in your tests?
   Is there anyone who hasn't returned their test?

2 • These phrases show position according to top and bottom of the page. Notice:

> five lines **down** = five lines **from the top**
> two lines **up** = two lines **from the bottom**

3 • When used adjectivally, the words 'left' and 'right' require the ending **-hand**:

> on the left ⇒ the left-hand side
> on the right ⇒ the right-hand page

• Notice the adjectival use of **top, bottom, centre** and **middle**:

> the bottom line
> the middle paragraph
> the top row

4 • Articles: Where ordinal numbers are used and they come first in the phrase or sentence, **no** definite article is necessary:

> Third paragraph or The third paragraph
> Fifth line or The fifth line

But: And now **the** third paragraph.
And not: ★ And now third paragraph.

Similarly:

last	(the) last paragraph
next	(the) next line
top	(the) top picture
bottom	(the) bottom row

1 **Have you found the place?**
   Do you know where we are?
   Have you all found the place?
   Is there anybody who (still) hasn't found the place?
   Show Bill the place
   Help Alison find the place

2 **It's at the bottom of the page**
   The picture at the top of the page/at the very top
   The line in the middle of the page
   It's somewhere near the top/bottom (of the page)
   It's towards the bottom/end
   It's about halfway down
   It's in the very middle of the page
   About three-quarters of the way down
   The top/bottom/middle line
   It's ten lines from the top/bottom
   Ten lines down/up
   (The) tenth line from the top/bottom
   (The) tenth line down/up
   (The) third row down/up

3 **It's on the left**
   It's on the right
   The left-hand side/the right-hand side
   It's in the top left-hand corner
   It's in the bottom right-hand corner
   It's in the left-hand margin
   Look at the right-hand column
   (The) third column (from the left/right)
   The centre/middle column
   The shaded area on the right
   Look at the coloured box underneath

4 **Paragraph three, line two**
   (The) third paragraph, (the) second line/sentence
   (The) last line of the first paragraph
   (The) last line in the second paragraph
   The paragraph beginning/starting/ending 'he said . . .'
   (The) last but one line/word in paragraph two
   (The) second/third to last word in line 5
   Line five, (the) seventh word
   (The) third line, (the) fourth word (along)
   About the middle of line 12

5 **A few lines further on**
   Five lines further down/up
   Not the next line, but the one after that
   Not the previous line, but the one before that
   (The) next but one sentence, (the) third word

6 D TEXTBOOK ACTIVITY

1 • Notice the following vocabulary:

Check:	Let's check what you have written
Check through:	Let's check through the answers
Check up:	I'll check this up in a dictionary
Check on:	Could you check on the spelling of it
Check off:	Check off the answers on your list

2 • First/at first: These phrases are often confused in the classroom. A simple rule: only use 'first' in the classroom, or its synonyms, **first of all, firstly, to start with**.

'At first' always suggests a contrast with later behaviour:

At first he was kind to me, **but then** he became cruel

'First' merely names the first action in a series of events:

First we shall sing, **and then** we shall work

Similarly, do not use 'at last' in the classroom, but **lastly** or **to finish with**.

• Future tense after 'first': First **we shall** try exercise 2. See Unit 9, section N4.

3 ★ The *ten first* lines.
Word order with 'first', 'next' and 'last'!
The first ten lines.

4 ★ *The* next.
Next.

'*This is a fine time to tell me you can't read.*'

1 **Read the passage silently**
   Read the text to yourselves
   Study the chapter on your own
   Prepare the next three paragraphs
   Have a look at the next section
   Check the new vocabulary from the list at the back
   If there are any words you don't know, please ask
   Familiarize yourselves with the text
   Read what it says at the top of the page first

2 **Let's read**
   Let's read the text aloud
   I'll read it to you first
   First of all, I'll read it to you
   You start (reading), Bill
   Alison will begin
   Start reading from line 6
   Read the sentence aloud
   Now we'll read it again. Bill, you can be Mr Brown
   Alison, you read the part of Mrs Brown this time
   Let's read the conversation again, with you Bill reading the part of Mr Brown
   Let's try it again, but this time with Alison as Mrs Brown

3 **Read the first ten lines**
   Read as far as/down to the end of the chapter
   Three lines each (starting with Bill)
   Three sentences for each of you
   Read one sentence each
   Let's take turns/it in turns to read/reading
   One after the other, please
   Another sentence, please
   Finish the sentence (off)
   Read to the end of line 5
   Don't stop in the middle of the sentence
   Stop there, please
   That's enough, thank you
   That will do (fine), thank you

4 **Go on reading, Bill**
   Read the next bit/section/paragraph, will you, Bill
   Next, please
   Next one, please
   You go on, Bill
   Someone else, please
   Alison, go on from where Bill left off

1 • Check the following vocabulary:

Do you know the meaning of the	word 'deceive'
	phrase 'out cold'
	idiom 'to be hand in glove'
	expression 'at a loss'
	saying 'it's an ill wind'
	words in italics
	words underlined
	letters 'UNESCO'
	abbreviation 'pm'
	initials 'PM'

★ Are there any questions *of* this text?
  Preposition: **on.**

★ Is there *still something* you want to ask?
  Is there anything else/more you want to ask?

• Note: ⎰ I am unfamiliar with this expression
         ⎱ This expression is unfamiliar to me

  ⎰ I'm still not clear about the difference
  ⎱ The difference is still not clear to me

2 • See also Unit 10, section P2.

★ Let's *pick up* the difficult points.
  Let's look at the difficult points.

★ I'd like to *point (at)* some difficulties.
  I'd like to point out some difficulties.

3 Notice the changes in accentuation:

adjective ['ædʒiktiv]	adjectival ['ædʒek'taivəl]
adverb ['ædvə:b]	adverbial [əd'və:biəl]

Hollowood

'What does festival mean, dad?'

1   **Do you understand everything?**
Is there anything you don't understand?
Do you know the meaning of all the words?
Are there any words you don't know the Finnish/French/ … for?
Are there any phrases you don't know the meaning of?
Can I help you with any words or phrases?
Are there any strange words or expressions?
Is everything clear?
Are there any questions on this text?
Has anybody got anything to ask (about this text)?
Is there anything else you would like to ask about?
Are there any points you're not sure of?
Are there any words you are unfamiliar with?
Would you like anything explained/explaining?

2   **We'll look at some difficult points in this text**
Let's have a look at some of the difficult points
Let's start with a look at the difficulties in this text
There are one or two difficult points we should look at
I'd like to point out some difficult constructions
Let's look at the passage in more detail
Perhaps we should have a detailed look at this again
This is a good opportunity to revise the past tense
Perhaps we can do some quick revision

3   **Look at line 4 for a moment**
If you look at line 4, you will notice that the adjective . . .
In line 4 you can see the word 'best'
Look at the first/last line of the first paragraph
Look at the end of the very first line
Second paragraph, first line, the word 'fast'
A little further down, about two lines from the bottom . . .
I'd like to draw your attention to the word 'drag' in line 26
It's worth noticing how the word 'sicken' is used in line 5
This means (more or less) the same as 'she left'
The meaning of this sentence is something like 'he didn't understand'

6 D TEXTBOOK ACTIVITY

1 ★ Answer *to* the *four first* questions.
  Answer the first four questions.

- Answer
  Verb: No preposition—**Answer my question/the question**
  Noun: +'to'—**What is the answer to this?**
  　　　+'for'—**What answer have you got for question 9?**

- Articles
  No article where cardinal number used:
  page 75, line 10, chapter 5
  Compulsory article for grammatical terms:
  in **the** plural; use **the** conditional

3 ★ I didn't *take any mistake* if you . . .
  I didn't take off any points if you . . .

- A list of possible instructions for various types of exercise is given in Unit 10, sections P7–8.

- Note the uses of the word **mark**:

  What **mark** did you get last time? (score)
  You lose a **mark** if you put 'go' (point)
  Mark your own tests (correct)
  Mark the right answer with a cross (show)

4 • How/what: these are often confused.
  How

  　—precedes a transitive verb with a separate object;
  　—precedes an intransitive verb:

  How should you write it?
  How do you answer the first question?
  How does number 5 go?
  How did you get on?

  What

  　—requires a transitive verb where 'what' is the object;
  　—precedes 'to be' as a complement:

  What did you write?
  What should you say?
  What is your answer?
  What was number 6?

See also Unit 10, exercise I.

1   **Try exercise 6**
   I want you to do exercise 7A
   Try the next exercise as well
   Answer the first four questions
   Answer every other question
   Let's go on to exercise number 2
   Do the whole of/part of/some of the exercise
   If you get stuck, skip the question
   If you get stuck on one, leave it out and come back to it later

2   **Let's go through this exercise**
   Let's go over the exercise together
   Let's go through the sentences on the board
   Let's check the answers
   Now we'll see how well you got on/went on/did
   Let's run through the answers quickly
   I think you are more or less ready, so let's see how you got on
   I'll return your tests now
   I'll give you your tests back and we can go through them together

3   **Check your answers on page 123**
   Mark your own
   Change papers with someone/your neighbour/partner
   The right answers are on page 123
   Give yourself one point for every correct answer
   One point for every one right
   Take off a point for every one (you got) wrong
   Count up your points
   How many did you get right/wrong?
   Did anybody get them all right?
   What was your score?/How many points did you score?
   Anybody with one mistake? Two mistakes?
   I didn't count it as a mistake if you put 'big'
   I didn't take any points off if you forgot to . . .

4   **What's the answer to number 1?**
   How does the first one go?
   What have you got for number 1?
   What do you have for question 9?
   What have you put/written/marked for question 11?
   Let's go on to number 2
   And the next one, please, Bill
   What about the last one, Alison?
   Could somebody read out what they put for number 2?
   Has anybody got anything for the last one?

'Please excuse scribble.'

2 • BLOCK LETTERS
   italics
   bold print

3 ★ Write the exercise out *on* your notebooks.
   Write the exercise out in your notebooks.

4 ★ 'With' is a preposition and requires a noun after it.
   Have you got a pen with you?

   • Notice the following items of classroom equipment:

   > a pen
   > a pencil
   > a ball-point pen
   > a biro ['bairou]
   > a felt-tip pen
   > a rubber
   > an eraser [i'reizə]
   > a ruler
   > a pencil case

1 **Copy this down in your notebooks**
  Take this down in your exercise books
  Put/take/get/write/copy that down
  Make a note of this somewhere/in your books
  Don't forget to write that down
  Write it in the margin
  Write it in the empty space at the top
  Underline the new words
  Jot this down somewhere so that you don't forget it

2 **Write it in block letters**
  Print it
  Write in in block capitals
  Write it in big letters

3 **Write it neatly**
  Write it out legibly at home
  Make sure I can read your handwriting
  Rewrite it neatly
  Your handwriting is illegible, Bill
  Write this exercise out neatly in your notebooks

4 **Do the exercise in pencil**
  Do the exercise in writing
  Try it in ink
  Rewrite it in ink
  Use a pen/pencil
  Has anybody got an extra pencil?
  Have you got a spare pen/pencil with/on you?
  Come out and sharpen your pencil
  Has anybody got a pencil sharpener on him/her?
  Could you lend Bill a pen or a pencil?

5 **We'll do the exercise orally**
  Let's try it aloud before you write it down

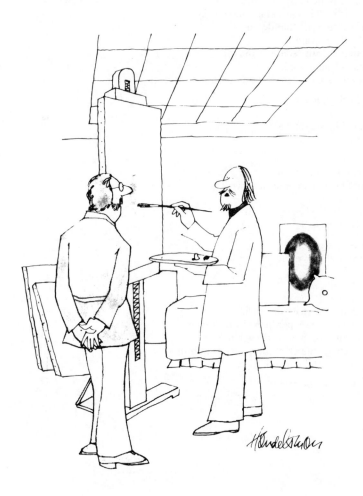

'*I would have preferred to write, but I had nothing to say.*'

1   **Take out your coloured pencils**
Take out your crayons
Take out your drawing things
Have you all got your coloured pencils with you?

2   **Let's draw some pictures**
Let's do some drawing
Now we'll do some colouring

3   **Colour the bus red**
Draw a bus and colour it red
Draw a cat and give it a black tail
Draw a house with a red door
Draw a dog. Now draw a black tail for it

1 ● Notice: To **act (out)**. Not: *to play*.
But: to **play the part of** Mr Brown.
And: Bill is in this **play**.

2 ● See also section D5, heading 2.

● Notice the transactional language pupils can use in preparing a dramatization or role play:

> it's my turn
> let's try it again
> shall we change over?
> that's not a very good idea
> what if I play the waiter?   etc.

See also: Maley and Duff, *Drama Techniques in Language Learning*, Cambridge 1978.

1 **Now let's act out this dialogue**
Now we shall act this conversation (out)
Let's watch Bill and Alison acting the conversation out
Let's see Bill and Alison's little play
Who would like to act the scene for us?
Come out to the front and show everybody else

2 **You be Mr Brown**
You are/will be Mrs Brown, Alison
You can read the part of Bill
Who wants to be Alice?
Who would like to read the part of Jack?
You are the prompter
The rest of you are the audience
You can be the reader, Alison

3 **Let's rehearse first**
Let's try it once with the book
This will be our dress rehearsal
You can use your book
Try to manage without your book

4 **Will the actors and actresses come out to the front**
I think we should clap
Some applause for the actors and actresses
Let's applaud the actors and actresses

5 **Pretend that you're a postman**
Imagine that you're phoning your brother
Try and act like a bus-conductor
Act as if you don't really care

6 EXERCISES

I. Fill in the gaps, using the prepositions 'at', 'in', 'on' and 'to':

All right, group one. Open your books ... (1) page 76. Now, ... (2) the left you can see a picture. Err, the picture ... (3) the top of the page, not the one ... (4) the middle. Have you all found it? Right. Now turn ... (5) page 63. ... (6) the top left-hand corner you can see another picture. I want you to compare these two pictures ... (7) detail. You'll find some ideas ... (8) your workbooks ... (9) page 145. You might also refer ... (10) the wordlist ... (11) the back ... (12) page 176. You can jot your ideas down ... (13) the margin. You will probably get some help from a short description ... (14) your textbook. If you turn for a moment ... (15) chapter 16, you'll see a short article by Bernard Shaw. Perhaps you could keep one finger ... (16) this section, and then you can refer back ... (17) it when necessary. Have a look especially ... (18) the last sentence ... (19) the second paragraph. When you finally get down to writing your comparison, write it ... (20) your exercise books ... (21) ink or biro. You can spend half an hour ... (22) this.

And now, group two. Take out your readers and open them ... (23) page 13. Finish off the work you were ... (24) last time, and then start reading chapter 4. If you look at line 5. Got it? Well, ... (25) line 5 there's the word 'tough'. I want you to try and find other words to describe James Bond. So, first read the text ... (26) yourself. You'll find a list of vocabulary ... (27) page 27 ... (28) the bottom ... (29) the empty space below the photograph. Write your list ... (30) the sheet of paper I'm going to give you, and this time please remember to write your name ... (31) it! Are there any questions ... (32) this?

II. By choosing an adverb particle and a verb from the two lists it is possible to complete the sentences.

Verbs: finish give go turn put leave look take hand collect count copy
Adverbs: away in off on out over round up

In certain cases more than one answer is possible.

1. As you leave, please remember to ... your summaries ....

2. Since there aren't enough copies to ... ..., you'll have to share.

3. Right. ... your points ... and then subtract from twenty. That will be your mark.

4. You won't be needing your workbook for the next few minutes, so you can ... it ....

5. Today we'll learn a song. Mary, could you ... the words ..., please. One between two.

6. I think it was chapter seven where we ... ... reading last time. So let's continue from there.

7. If there are any points you're not sure of, you can ... them ... in the grammar section on page 210, or you can ask me.

8. That wasn't an easy test. It'll be interesting to see how you ... . You should all have got five right at least.

9. If you forgot the comma after 'however', I didn't ... ... a point this time. But I will next time, so be warned.

10. Would you please ... ... the sentence you're doing at the moment and then put your pens down.

11. Now that we've read the text, you can ... your books .... That's right, all books face down please.

12. Ali, would you please ... ... the test papers and bring them to me so that I can mark them.

13. I think we ought to ... ... this exercise again before starting exercise 7. There were a few tricky points we ought to look at.

14. I suggest we ... ... with the project work until half past.

15. There weren't many mistakes, but perhaps you could ... ... the last paragraph again. Do it in your exercise books and use a clean page.

III. Fill in the definite article wherever it is possible in the following sentences. Put brackets ( ) around those that may be left out.

1. Open your books at ... page 23, ... chapter 10.

2. Do we need ... past or would it be better to use ... past perfect?

3. All right. ... third paragraph, ... second line, ... word 'save'.

4. Answer ... first four questions, would you, please.

5. How about ... sentence number five? Jan, what have you put for ... number five?

6. No, not ... next line, but ... second to last line.

7. ... next, please. It's your turn, isn't it, Erika?

8. I think the verb has to be in ... plural, too.

9. ... next sentence, please. Yes, that's right, ... question 7.

10. Right. Now say ... same thing, using ... passive.

6 EXERCISES

IV. Describe the position of the numbered places and words, etc., by completing the sentences below.

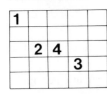

1. The picture in the t... l...-h... corner.

2. It's in the t... row d..., second f... the l....

3. The s... row from the b..., the l... but one picture.

4. It's in the v... middle.

5. The paragraph at the t... of the page.

6. It's t... the end of the third paragraph.

7. It's about h... d... the page.

8. It's at the v... b... of the page.

9. The f... p..., second l..., s... word.

10. Two l... from the e... of paragraph one, the third t... l... word.

11. The s... to l... line of paragraph two, the sixth word a....

12. The f... t... words of p... t....

13. No, not the first line, but t... lines f... d....

14. Not the next line, but the o... a... t....

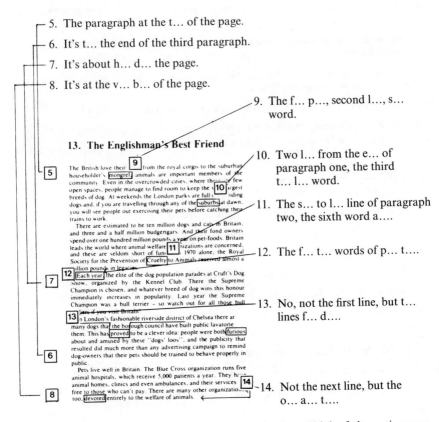

13. The Englishman's Best Friend

The British love their [9] from the royal corgis to the suburban householder's [mongrel] animals are important members of the community. Even in the overcrowded cities, where there are few open spaces, people manage to find room to keep the v[10] rgest breeds of dog. At weekends the London parks are full of riding dogs and, if you are travelling through any of the [suburbs] at dawn, you will see people out exercising their pets before catching their trains to work.

There are estimated to be ten million dogs and cats in Britain, and three and a half million budgerigars. And their fond owners spend over one hundred million pounds a year on pet-foods. Britain leads the world where animal welfare [11] nizations are concerned, and these are seldom short of fun... 1970 alone, the Royal Society for the Prevention of [Cruelty] to Animals received almost a million pounds in legacies.

[12] Each year the elite of the dog population parades at Cruft's Dog Show, organized by the Kennel Club. There the Supreme Champion is chosen, and whatever breed of dog wins this honour immediately increases in popularity. Last year the Supreme Champion was a bull terrier – so watch out for all those bull ts if you visit Britain.

[13] n London's fashionable riverside district of Chelsea there are many dogs that the borough council have built public lavatories for them. This has [proved] to be a clever idea: people were both [furious] about and amused by these "dogs' loos", and the publicity that resulted did much more than any advertising campaign to remind dog-owners that their pets should be trained to behave properly in public.

Pets live well in Britain. The Blue Cross organization runs five animal hospitals, which receive 5,000 patients a year. They h... animal homes, clinics and even ambulances, and their services [14] free to those who can't pay. There are many other organizations, too, [devoted] entirely to the welfare of animals.

Now repeat the exercise, but this time do not use the clues. Think of alternative ways of describing the same positions.

V. Work in fours. Each person has a copy of the same textbook. One person describes the precise location of a single word (page, paragraph, line, word number) and the others try to find it. The first one to do so gets a point. A point is lost if the description is inaccurate.

VI. The passage below is a description of an English lesson. At the places numbered, e.g. (1), the teacher might say something appropriate in English. What does the teacher say?

You've got a lot of work to get through in this lesson. The first task is on page 97. You ask the pupils to open their books (1). Some of them look rather mystified, so you check that they do in fact have their books with them (2). You're annoyed because some of them have left their books at home again (3). Carmen and Maria have only one book between them (4). You check that they all have the right place (5). You make sure that there aren't any new words in the next section (6), and then you ask Carlos to read three lines (7). He obviously can't count and you have to stop him (8). Now you want everybody to read three lines each. You choose Jessica to start (9).

The passage was about sport in Britain and you decide to give them some background information. They should listen and make notes in their exercise books (10). After that they will need their workbooks, page 43 (11). Exercise 14A is still incomplete (12). When everybody appears to have completed the exercise (13), you stop them (14) and check the exercise (15). You ask the following pupils for the answers: number 6— Selma, (16), number 7—Orlando, (17), number 8—Federico, (18) and the last one—Garcia (19). You decide to start the next exercise, which is a defective dialogue. It seems best to try it once before the pupils write it down (20), but they will have to write a fair copy at home (21). In the next lesson they will also have to dramatise their dialogues for the other pupils (22).

In the remaining five minutes, you have a quick vocabulary test. As the bell rings, you ask them to return the completed test papers and to make it clear who they belong to (23).

VII. Role-play the situations described in exercise VI. Use some of the earlier exercises in this unit as your lesson material. Remember to vary the form of your requests for answers.

6 ANSWERS

I 1. at 2. on 3. at 4. in 5. to 6. in 7. in 8. in 9. on 10. to 11. at
12. on 13. in 14. in 15. to 16. in 17. to 18. at 19. in 20. in
21. in 22. on 23. at 24. on 25. in 26. to 27. on 28. at 29. in
30. on 31. on 32. on

II 1. hand/leave in 5. give out 9. take off 13. go over
2. go round 6. left/finished off 10. finish off 14. go on
3. count up 7. look up 11. turn over 15. copy out
4. put away 8. went on 12. collect in/up

III 1. —, — 3. (the), the), the 5. —, — 7. — 9. (the), —
2. the the 4. the 6. the, the 8. the 10. the, the

IV 1. The picture in the *top left-hand* corner.
2. It's in the *third* row *down*, second *from* the *left*.
3. The *second* row from the *bottom*, the *last* but one picture.
4. It's in the *very* middle.
5. The paragraph at the *top* of the page.
6. It's *towards* the end of the third paragraph.
7. It's about *halfway down* the page.
8. It's at the *very bottom* of the page.
9. The *first paragraph*, second *line*, *second* word.
10. Two *lines* from the *end* of paragraph one, the third *to last* word.
11. The *second* to *last* line of paragraph two, the sixth word *along*.
12. The *first two* words of *paragraph three*.
13. No, not the first line, but *two* lines *further down*.
14. Not the next line, but the *one after that*.

V Suggested answers

1. Open your books at page 97, please.
2. Is there anybody who hasn't got a book?
3. Please try to remember it next time.
4. Carmen, could you share with Maria, please?
5. Have you all found the place?
6. Are there any words or expressions that you are unfamiliar with?
7. Carlos, would you read the first three lines, please.
8. That will do, thank you.
9. Three lines each, please, starting with Jessica.
10. Make notes on what I say in your exercise books.
11. Now, could you take out your workbooks and open them at page 43.
12. I want you to finish off exercise 14A.
13. Well, everybody seems to be more or less ready.
14. All right, I think you've had long enough on this. Stop writing, please.
15. Let's go through the exercise together.
16. What was the answer to number 6? Selma, please.
17. And what have you got for number 7, Orlando?
18. And how does number 8 go? What about you, Federico?
19. And now the last one. What did you put for that, Garcia?
20. Let's try and do it orally first.
21. It would be a good idea for you to copy the dialogue out at home.
22. Next time I want you to act out your dialogues for the rest of the class.
23. Hand in your papers as you leave and make sure your names are on them.

Unit 7

'*Father's never ceased to be amazed at the phenomenon of electricity.*'

1 • The choice between 'come' and 'go' will naturally depend on the teacher's own position.

3 • Notice that you **write something up** on the blackboard.
Also note:

> Please **write** this **down** in your books
> **Write** this **out** again at home
> **Write up** these notes at home

'*Don't worry, Sire. I'll get someone else for the legs.*'

1 **Come out to the blackboard, please**
Go to the board
Go up to the blackboard
Come and stand by the blackboard

2 **You have already been out to the board**
Who hasn't been out to the blackboard yet?
Whose turn is it to write the sentence up?

3 **Come and write the word on the board**
Come out and write that sentence on the board
Write that on the board
Write it here/there
Write it next to/above/below that word
Take a piece of chalk and write the sentence out
Here's a piece of chalk. Write it up on the board
Try and keep your writing straight/level

4 **Come out and draw a cat on the blackboard**

5 **Move out of the way so that everyone can see**
Step aside so that the class can see what you have written
Move to one side so that we can all see
Push the board up a bit
You'll have to lower the board slightly

6 **Go and fetch some chalk from the office**
I've run out of chalk
Go and see if there's any next door
Go and ask Mr Smith for some (pieces of) chalk
Would you go and look for some chalk for me, please
Does anyone know where the chalk is kept?
Do you know if there's any coloured chalk?

3 ★   *Let's take the sentences again* and *Let's take it again* are common errors.
In English the precise nature of the task must be given:

> Let's **listen** to the conversation again
> Let's **try** it again
> We can **read** this again
> I want you to **do** number 7 again
> Let's go through it again

5 ★   *Take this away.*
Rub this off.

Notice the uses of **out, off** and **away**:

> Please **rub** this **out/off**
> **Take** your books **out**
> You can **leave out** the relative
> **Turn** the lights **out/off**, would you
> **Put** your books **away**

1 **Everyone look at the blackboard, please**
Everybody look at the board
Let's look at the sentences on the board
Look at the pattern on the board

2 **Are the sentences on the board right?**
Are there any mistakes in the sentences on the board?
Can you see anything wrong with the sentences?
Anything wrong with sentence 5?
Rub out the wrong word
Wipe out/off the last letter
Rub that off
Is there anything to correct in sentence 3?

3 **Read out the sentences on the blackboard**
Bill, read the first sentence
Let's all read the sentences from the board
We'll read them again, but this time all together
Look at the model/pattern on the board and ask questions

4 **Copy this down from the blackboard**
I'll write up the correct answers on the board
I want you to copy the questions down in your notebooks
Copy this straight down into your notebooks
Make a note of the last two sentences
Try to note/jot down the new words as we go along

5 **Whose turn is it to clean the board?**
Who is the monitor?
Clean the board, please, Bill
We can wipe this last exercise off now
Use the duster/sponge
Wet the sponge under the tap
You can wipe this line off
You can leave that exercise up
Leave the answers on the board
There's no need to rub that exercise off

1

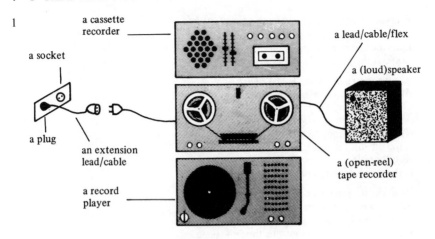

- The use of **seem to** is typically English in this sort of situation.
3
- Suitably mild complaints include:

> Dear me! Oh dear! Blast! Blow (me)! Curse! Hell!

★ *I can't help.*
There's nothing I can do (about it).

4

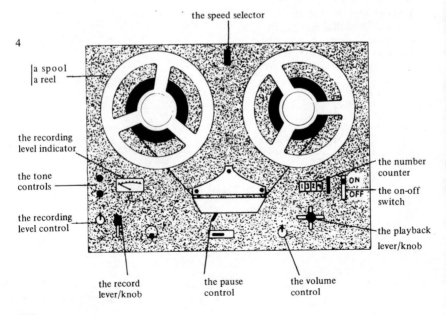

1   **Mind the tape recorder**
Don't trip over the tape recorder lead
Mind the cable when you go out
Careful where you're stepping

2   **Could you plug the recorder in, please**
Turn it on/off
Switch it on/off
Put this plug in the socket over there
Unplug the recorder
Pull the plug out of the wall

3   **The tape recorder seems to be broken**
There's/there seems to be something wrong (with it)
The recorder isn't working properly
I have/seem to have brought the wrong tape
We'll have to do something else, I'm afraid
There's nothing we can do about it
There's nothing to be done
Do any of you know anything about tape recorders?
Does anyone know how this works?
I can't find the switch

4   **Can you all hear?**
Is it clear enough?
Is the sound clear enough?
Is the volume all right?
Can you hear at the back?
If you can't hear, come a bit nearer
Is that better?
I've got too much treble and not enough bass

5   **I'll just find the place**
Wait a moment/second/minute, I'll just rewind the tape
Let me just find the beginning again
Look at the questions while I find the place

6   **I'm sorry about that**
I'm sorry about the mix-up over the tapes
I'll try not to let it happen again
Sorry about the delay

1 ★ *At first.*
  First of all. (See Unit 9, section N4, heading 3.)

2 ★ *Let's take it again.*
  Let's listen to it/do it again.

  When followed by an object, the verb 'listen' requires the preposition **to**:

Listen carefully! but: Listen **to me** carefully
Listen now   but: Listen **to this** now

'He's saving up for a longer flex.'

1 **Let's listen to the tape now**
First of all, listen to the conversation
Now you'll hear the conversation
You can hear the sentences on the tape
What you will hear is a conversation
Here goes
Off we go then
Here it comes

2 **Listen again**
Let's listen to it once more/once again
Now we'll listen to it again
We have enough time to listen to it again
We'll stop here/there for a moment
Before we go on, I'll ask you some questions

3 **Listen and repeat**
All together, after the tape
Repeat after the tape

4 **Just listen**
Just listen. Don't say anything
Listen but don't write anything
Listen carefully to the instructions

5 **As you listen, do exercise 5**
As you listen, fill in the missing words
While you listen/you are listening, answer question 2
While listening, mark your answer sheet
Before listening, read through the questions
Before listening again, familiarize yourselves with the questions

6 **Now I have a pop song for you**
Listen to the words of the song
Try to follow what the singer is saying
Here's a song by Simon and Garfunkel called 'Cecilia'

1. ● Notice:

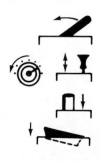

a lever ['liːvə]: to pull/push a lever

a knob [nɔb]: to pull/push/turn a knob

a button: to press/push a button

a switch: to press/flick a switch

Modern usage is quite loose and the words are often used interchangeably.

● Notice:

to turn the recorder	on
	up (= louder)
	down (= softer)
	off
to adjust the volume (= up or down)	

2 ● Any of the following might happen:

I've snapped the tape
The tape has got tangled up
The tape has got snarled up inside somewhere
The tape was the wrong way round
The fuse has gone/blown
I'll have to rethread the tape

John Copeland

'Actually I'm only really learning German to flatten my ears.'

1 **Check your controls**
   Check your microphone is switched on
   Make sure your number counter is at zero
   Have you got enough tape on the left-hand spool?
   Move the channel selector switch to the 'Student' position
   Adjust the volume
   Turn the volume up/down
   Make sure you pull down both levers/knobs when recording
   Are your microphone and earphone plugs the right way round?
   Press your calling button if you have any problems
   Is your headset working?
   Don't put the microphone directly in front of your mouth

2 **Can everybody hear?**
   Is there anybody who can't hear me/the group/the programme?
   Is there anybody having trouble?
   Did you remember to pull the recording lever, too?
   Have you switched your microphone on?
   Could you move to an empty booth. Number 16 is free
   Number 10 is out of order. Try number 11
   You'll have to listen in with Alison
   I'll switch you into Bill's programme
   Plug your headphones into the free socket
   Don't mess around/fiddle with the controls

3 **Please get ready to record**
   I'll play the programme from the console
   You can record it on your own recorders/tapes
   After recording, you can go back and listen to it again
   Rewind your tapes and listen again
   Go back to the beginning and re-record your answers
   Rewind and try the exercise again
   Stop the tape as many times as you want/wish

4 **I shall now join you up in(to) groups**
   You will be connected up with someone else in the class

5 **Go back and try again**
   Go back and listen to what you said. Then try again
   There was a mistake in that sentence. Go back and see if you can find/spot it

6 **Remember to sign the record book**
   Put your name, today's date and the time
   Fill in the laboratory register
   Hang up your headphones before you leave
   Hang your headphones up with the microphone away from the wall
   Don't leave your headset on the desk

7 G SLIDES, PICTURES, OHP

1 • Remember: **to look at**, but also:

Look this way!	but not: ★ Look at here
Look!	★ Look here
Look over there!	

Look here is to be considered abrupt and perhaps rude in this situation, but is possible in other circumstances. See Unit 8, section K.

2 ★ *Open/close* the projector.
Switch the projector on/off.

Notice:

Please	turn	the lights	on
	put	the radio	off
	switch	the recorder	

3 ★ *Take* the plug *off*.
Pull the plug out.

4 • Notice the various types of visual aid:

an overhead transparency
  ['ouvəhed træns'pærənsi]
an overhead
an OHP
a slide
a transparency
a filmstrip
a poster
a wallchart
a cutout

1 **Let's look at some pictures**
Now we're going to look at some (colour) slides
I want you to look at this picture
I'm going to show you some slides of England
I have a film to show you today
There's a diagram I'd like to show you on the OHP

2 **Put the screen up**
Draw the curtains
Close the blinds
Pull down the screen
Plug in the projector
Switch on the projector
Switch the lights off
Lights out, please
Who is our projectionist today?
Who is going to change the pictures?
Who would like to work/operate the projector?
Pass me my pointer

3 **Turn the lights on again**
Put the lights back on
Pull the plug out
Unplug the projector
Roll up the screen
Put the screen away
Draw the curtains

4 **Next picture, please**
Let's look at the next one
Change the picture
Let's go on to the next one
Adjust the focus, please
A bit sharper, please
I'm afraid this one is upside down/back to front
I seem to have put this one in the wrong way round
Hang on, I'll put it in again

5 **The projector doesn't seem to be working**
The bulb has gone/burnt out
The slide cartridge seems to be stuck again
Same old trouble again, I'm afraid
The automatic focusing has gone wrong

2 ★ A picture *from* a railway station.
   A picture of a railway station.

 ★ A photograph *about* Bill and Alison.
   A photograph of Bill and Alison.

 ★ *On* this picture.
   In this picture.

 • Notice also that you say 'an example **of** something'.
   Compare:

> This is **a film about** London—Here is **a picture of** London
> I have **some brochures about** Wales—Here is **a slide of** Snowdon
> **A book about** England—**A description of** England
> Some **stories about** his temper—An **example of** his temper

Notice the following useful commentary phrases:

The first slide I want	to show you you to look at	is of a famous . . . was taken in . . . is a good example of . . . will give you some idea of what . . . will help you understand more about . . .

In this one you can see	some typically English scenery a view from Ben Nevis a typical London street scene

Additional, more advanced phrases useful in showing slides can be found on page 136.

3 • **Show me** and **point to it** follow when the teacher says: 'Is there a cat in the picture?', for example.

 ★ You cannot merely say *Show*.
   Show me./Show it to me.

 • **Point at** tends to be used in sentences like the following:

> He **pointed his finger at** me
> **Point your pencil at** the board

 • **To point something out:**

> Can anybody **point out** the mistake in sentence 2?
> I should **point out** that you need the passive in the last sentence
> Come and **point out** Bristol and Liverpool for me

5 ★ I'll let this *pass*.
   I'll pass this round.

1 **Everyone, look at the screen**
   Look at the picture
   Can you all see?
   Sit somewhere where you can see

2 **This is a picture of a railway station**
   This picture is of an English pub
   This is a photograph of Bill and Alison
   In this picture you can see an English school
   This picture shows part of the British Museum

3 **Show me the cat**
   Point to the cat
   Show me where the cat is in this picture
   Show me
   Point to it
   Come out and point to England on the map

4 **I'll ask you some questions about the picture**
   Ask your friend some questions about it
   What can you see in the picture?
   Tell me what you can see
   What can you say about the picture?
   What is there in the corner/background?
   What is happening in this picture?
   Describe some of the people in the picture

5 **Pass this picture round**
   I'll let this photograph go round
   I'll pass this book round
   Have a look and then pass it on

6 **Come out and write the answer (on the overhead projector)**
   Come and write the answer on the overhead transparency
   Here's a felt-tip pen. Come and write your answer down

Additional phrases

1. **Apologizing for the quality of pictures**
   It's not awfully clear, I'm afraid
   It's not very sharp
   It's a bit out of focus
   I'm sorry about the colours
   There was probably something wrong with the film
   This one is rather underexposed/overexposed
   I was in a bit of a hurry when I took this
   This was taken on a very cloudy day

2. **Directing attention to particular features**
   If you look carefully to the right of the shop, you'll see . . .
   Can you make out the library, just to the left of the church?
   See if you can pick out the shopkeeper
   Have a good/close look at the man standing in the boat
   Of particular interest in this picture is the food they're eating
   What is interesting about this picture is the costume
   Pay attention especially to the way the girl is dancing
   Even if you look at nothing else, I think it's worth looking at . . .

3. **Position of objects/persons in pictures**
   On the left/right
   On the far left/left-hand side
   At the very edge of the picture
   At the top/bottom
   In the top/bottom left/right-hand corner
   To the left of the white building
   Just a bit/immediately to the right of the church
   In the (very) middle/centre of the picture
   In the foreground/background
   Just beyond the hill
   On the far/near bank of the river
   On this/the other side of the square
   On the brow of the hill
   At the far end of the street

4. **General purpose phrases and questions**
   In fact, this next one is quite an interesting picture because . . .
   Well, believe it or not, I took the next picture
   Ah, this is another example of my photographic genius
   If I remember correctly, this one was taken in Australia/on the side of Mount Everest
   Has anybody any idea what this (thing/person) is called?
   Do you notice anything odd/strange/unusual about this picture?
   What time of day do you think it was taken? How do you know?
   In which season was this picture taken? How can you tell?
   Talking of churches, how many churches are there . . .?
   While we're on the subject of airports, have any of you ever been to . . .?
   This picture reminds me of a story I heard about a man who . . .
   By the way, could somebody read out what it says on the notice
   In passing, perhaps I ought to point out that farming in England . . .

I. Complete the following sentences, using the prepositions and adverbs in the list:

away   down   of   off   out   in   from

1. Pardon? It's too loud, you say. I'm sorry, I'll turn it ....

2. Next picture. Aah, yes, this is a photograph ... a London bus that passed me in Oxford Street.

3. Somebody might trip over this cable, so John, could you please pull it ....

4. Alain, you pull the blinds ..., and Marie, you switch the lights ....

5. All right, please put your textbooks ... and take ... your workbooks.

6. In this case the relative pronoun can be left ... because this word is the object of the verb.

7. You are nearest the wall, Lin, so perhaps you could plug the tape recorder lead ....

8. Is there anything wrong with this sentence? Yes, I have to rub ... one of the 't's.

9. Could you copy these sentences ... ... the board.

10. Shoko, you've left the tap running. Please turn it ....

II. Fill in the gaps, using an appropriate word or phrase from the list.

a) headset
b) monitor
c) been out to
d) adjust
e) unplug
f) stand aside
g) wet
h) zero
i) pass round
j) upside down
k) work
l) booth
m) switch off
n) calling button
o) projectionist
p) slide
q) fuse
r) draw the curtains
s) rewind
t) screen

1. OK. Let's have a look at the first .... No, it wasn't taken in Australia, it's just ... . I'll put it in properly.

2. No, not you again Andreas. You've already ... ... the board once, haven't you?

3. This is a real mystery. I've checked all the controls, but it still doesn't .... The only thing I can think is that the ... has gone.

4. I'd like to show you a film now, so could you, Jussi, ..., and Tiina, could you put up the ....

5. I have some pictures of London I'd like to ... . Have a quick look at them and then give them to the person behind you. That's the way.

6. That's the end of the programme, so ... your tape until you come to ... on the counter, and then try the exercise again.

7. There may be something wrong with that ..., so take your ... off and hang it up, and then move to number 16. That should be all right.

8. ... the volume if you find it too loud. That's the knob on the left. And if you have any other problems, please press your ... . OK?

9. Who is the ... this week? Jean, you are, aren't you? All right. Well, ... the sponge and then clean the board.

10. Let's see what you've written. You'll have to ... otherwise nobody will be able to see.

III. The word 'point' has many uses. Read through the following sentences and then re-express the parts in **bold type**, using 'point'. A dictionary may be useful.

1. **Show me** where England is on this map.
2. What was your **score**?
3. I **mentioned** this problem in the last lesson, too.
4. If I remember correctly, we were **about to** begin a new chapter last time.
5. You should **try very hard** to learn these rules by heart.
6. I don't think you have really **understood the main idea** of this passage.
7. **It's a waste of time** starting exercise 7.
8. **What is** the mistake in sentence 5? **Anybody?**

IV. Translate the teacher's thoughts into words, using 'seem'.
Example:

'They haven't understood'
= You don't seem to have understood

Notice the English preference for saying 'don't seem' (cf. 'don't think', Unit 4, exercise II)

1. 'They haven't bothered to learn the vocabulary.'
2. 'Oh no, I haven't brought the tape with me!'
3. 'I knew this would happen. I can't find the place.'
4. 'That's all I need. Something wrong with the tape-recorder.'
5. 'They're all falling asleep.'
6. 'Don't tell me there's no writing paper left!'
7. 'They've forgotten everything I ever taught them about the conditional.'
8. 'Thank heavens there's not enough time to start exercise 5.'
9. 'They're not finding these exercises very easy.'
10. 'I'm not very good with anything mechanical.'

V. Two trainee teachers have been given the task of watching an English lesson given by a third trainee, and making notes on the lesson. They are to pay particular attention to any unexpected difficulties encountered and to the way the teacher copes with them.

On the sheet below you can see the original lesson plan, together with the two trainees' notes and comments

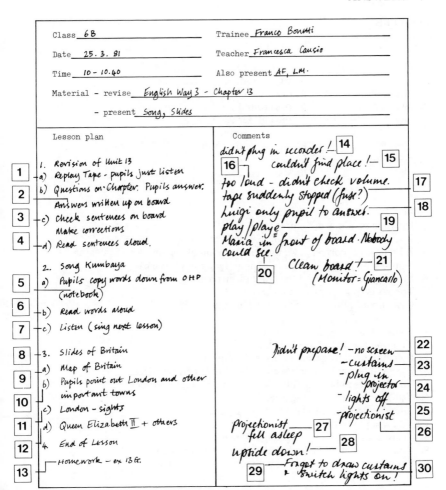

Class 6 B — Trainee Franco Bonetti

Date 25. 3. 81 — Teacher Francesca Causio

Time 10 – 10.40 — Also present AF, LM.

Material – revise English Way 3 – Chapter 13

— present Song, Slides

Lesson plan	Comments
1. Revision of Unit 13	didn't plug in recorder! **14**
1 a) Replay Tape – pupils just listen	**16** couldn't find place! – **15**
2 b) Questions on Chapter. Pupils answer.	too loud – didn't check volume. **17**
Answers written up on board	tape suddenly stopped (fuse?) **18**
3 c) Check sentences on board	Luigi only pupil to answer.
Make corrections	play/playe **19**
4 d) Read sentences aloud.	Maria in front of board. Nobody could see. **21**
2. Song Kumbaya	Clean board! – **21**
5 a) Pupils copy words down from OHP	**20** (Monitor = Giancarlo)
(notebook)	
6 b) Read words aloud	
7 c) Listen (sing next lesson)	
8 3. Slides of Britain	Didn't prepare! – no screen **22**
9 a) Map of Britain	– curtains **23**
b) Pupils point out London and other	– plug in projector **24**
10 important towns	– lights off **25**
11 c) London – sights	– projectionist **26**
12 d) Queen Elizabeth II + others	projectionist fell asleep **27**
4. End of Lesson	**28**
13 Homework – ex 13 G.	upside down! – **28**
	29 Forgot to draw curtains & switch lights on! **30**

Imagine now that you have to give the same lesson and that you encounter the same
problems. First of all, give the instructions for the different parts of the lesson
(numbered 1–13). Then find an appropriate apology or instruction for the problems
encountered (numbered 14–30).

VI Choose four slides or postcards and give a commentary on them. With the first
picture, concentrate on describing what there is in the picture. With the second one try
to give the position of things accurately. You can use the third one for talking about
how and when the picture was taken. And the last one can be the starting point for
an anecdote or joke.

VII Broadcast a 5-minute language laboratory drill, giving all your instructions
in English.

ANSWERS

I	II
1. down	1. slide, upside down
2. of	2. been out to
3. out	3. work, fuse
4. down, out/off	4. draw the curtains, screen
5. away, out	5. pass round
6. out	6. rewind, zero
7. in	7. booth, headset
8. out/off	8. adjust, calling button
9. down from	9. monitor, wet
10. off	10. stand aside

III
1. Point to England on this map.
2. How many points did you get/score?
3. I pointed out this problem in the last lesson, too.
4. If I remember correctly, we were on the point of beginning a new chapter last time.
5. You should make a point of learning these rules by heart.
6. I think you have missed the point of this passage.
7. There's no point (in) starting exercise 7.
8. Can anyone point out the mistake in sentence 5?

IV
1. You don't seem to have bothered to learn the vocabulary.
2. I seem to have forgotten to bring the tape with me.
3. I seem to be unable/don't seem to be able to find the place.
4. There seems to be something wrong with the tape-recorder.
5. You all seem to be falling asleep.
6. There doesn't seem to be any writing paper left.
7. You seem to have forgotten everything I ever taught you about the conditional.
8. There doesn't seem to be enough time to start exercise 5.
9. You don't seem to be finding these exercises very easy.
10. I don't seem to be very good with anything mechanical.

V. Suggested answers

1. Let's listen to the tape now. Just listen, don't repeat.
2. Come and write your answer on the board, please.
3. Are the sentences on the board right? Can anyone see anything wrong?
4. Now let's all read the sentences from the board.
5. I want you to copy the words of the song down in your notebooks.
6. Let's read out the words of the song.
7. Just listen and try to follow the words.
8. Today I'm going to show you some slides of Britain.
9. This is a map of Britain.
10. Come out and point to London on the map.
11. The next slide I want to show you is of Buckingham Palace in London.
12. And in this one you can see Queen Elizabeth.
13. Your homework for next time is exercise 13G.
14. Could you plug the tape-recorder in, please.
15. Wait a moment. I'll just find the place.
16. Is that loud enough? Can you all hear?
17. Oh dear. There seems to be something wrong with the tape-recorder. Perhaps the fuse has gone.
18. Luigi, you have already been out to the board. Who hasn't been out to the board yet?
19. Wipe off the last letter.
20. Move out of the way, Maria, so that everyone can see.
21. You're the monitor, aren't you, Giancarlo? Could you clean the board, please.
22. Pull down the screen, somebody.
23. Could you draw the curtains, please.
24. Would you mind plugging the projector in.
25. Switch the lights off.
26. Who would like to work the projector today?
27. Next picture, please.
28. I seem to have put it in upside down.
29. Draw the curtains somebody, please.
30. Put the lights back on, would you.

Unit 8

H Games and Songs

J Movement, General Activity

K Class Control

8 H GAMES AND SONGS

1 ● Popular games usually have a name, such as Blind Man's Buff, Hangman, Simon Says, I Spy with My Little Eye, etc. Most textbooks have a Teacher's Handbook with lists of games. See also: Lee, W. R., *Language Teaching Games and Contests*, Oxford University Press, 1977, and Chamberlain, Anthony and Kurt Stenberg, *Play and Practise!* John Murray, 1976.

2 ● In dividing themselves up into teams, English children sometimes use the following rhymes. The child indicated when the last phrase or word is spoken is either 'out' or put in a certain team:

> Eeny-meeny-miny-mo ['i:ni: 'mi:ni: 'maini: 'mou]
> Catch a tinker by the toe
> When he squeals, let him go
> Eeny-meeny-miny-mo
>
> One potato, two potato, three potato, four,
> Five potato, six potato, seven potato, more
>
> Dip, dip, dip, my blue ship,
> Sailing on the water like a cup and saucer,
> Dip, dip, dip, my blue ship

4 ● **Heads or tails?** is used when a coin is tossed. The condition can also be mentioned: Heads this team starts, tails Bill's team starts.

● **On your marks,** etc. Used for starting races (e.g. to the blackboard).

1 **Let's play a game**
   Now we'll play a guessing game
   What about a game of 'Simon Says'?
   Do you feel like a game now?
   Let's play a spelling/miming/guessing/counting game
   This is a game with colours/numbers/letters
   For this game we have to blindfold somebody
   Let's have a quiz
   The idea of this game is (for you) to score as many points as possible
   What you have to do is to guess . . .

2 **Get into two teams**
   Form two teams
   Get into five teams of four or five
   These two rows are one team
   All these boys and girls are in the other team
   Bill and Alison, you can pick your own teams
   I shall be the referee
   You can keep the score, Bill

3 **Now it's your turn to come out, Alison**
   You guessed right, so now you come out and ask
   Now you can be the question asker
   All right, one more
   That's the last time, I'm afraid

4 **Are you ready?**
   Heads or tails?
   On your marks. Get set. Go!

5 **Guess what this is**
   Guess what I am drawing
   Can anyone guess what this is/what I'm holding?
   I'll give you three guesses to find out what is in the basket
   You have three guesses to find out what is under my desk
   Ask the other children: 'Is it a book?'

1 • Both are correct: A point **to** the girls, a point **for** the girls.

 • Articles: Notice the use of the definite article in the following sentences:

> All right, boys
> Be quiet, girls!
> Tell **the** boys what you said
> A point for **the** girls

 ★ *Others*, don't help him.
 The others, don't help him. Definite article required.

3 • In games where the number of pupils taking part is gradually reduced, the teacher can say 'You're out' or 'Bill's out'.

 • In saying 'The winner', the teacher will point to the winner, or hold up his hand.

1 **One point for this team**
Two points for the girls
A point to the girls
The one who answers first will get a point
The first one to answer gets a point
The first one to write the word on the board scores a point
The first team with/to score ten points wins
You lose a point if you answer wrong

2 **Add up your points**
How many points have you got/did you get altogether?
What was your final score?
Let's count up the points together

3 **This team has won**
The winner!
The winning team!
It's a draw/tie
Three cheers for the winner. Hip-hip-hurray!
It was a close finish
Team A/Bill is the winner

4 **Let's sing**
Do you want to sing now?
How about a song?
First, I'll explain the words to you
Let's listen to the tune first
You already know this tune
It's the same tune as 'Up and Down'
Say the words after me
Do you know the words by heart yet?
Join in the singing, Bill
Once again, all together
Sing along with the children on the tape
I'll accompany you on my guitar
If you don't know the words, just hum

2 • Notice the prepositions:

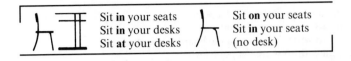

Sit **in** your seats	Sit **on** your seats
Sit **in** your desks	Sit **in** your seats
Sit **at** your desks	(no desk)

3

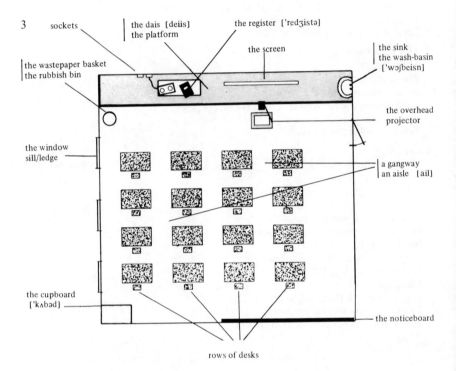

rows of desks

6 • Notice: **to pick up** cannot be used in the sense of going through a passage and looking at the new vocabulary. In such cases you would say:

Let's **have a look at** the new words
Let's **pick out** some of the difficult words

See Unit 10, section P2.

1 **Come in–Go out**
   Come inside
   Go outside
   Stay outside (for a moment)
   Go out and we will call you (back) in

2 **Stand up–Sit down**
   Stand by your desk(s)
   Sit in your seat(s)
   Stay in your seat(s)/place(s)
   Take your seats

3 **Come out to the front of the class**
   Come out (here) and face the class
   Come here
   I'd like to speak to you for a moment, Bill
   Could I have a word with you about your test, Alison
   Face the class/the board/me
   Look at the class
   Back to the class
   Turn your back to the class
   Stand with your back to the class

3 **Go and stand by the window**
   Go and sit at the back of the class
   Come and sit at the front
   Go and sit next to Bill   ·
   Take your seat and go and sit behind Alison
   You will have to go and sit next to someone else

5 **Now go and sit down again**
   Go back to your seat(s) please
   Thank you, you can sit down again
   Back to your place

6 **Come and fetch your book**
   Pick your book up off the floor
   Pick it up now
   Take this to Bill
   Give this book to Alison

1 ● Usage tends to favour the plural form with words like 'hand', 'book' etc., but the singular is also acceptable. It depends very much whether the teacher considers he is addressing the whole class or the individuals that together form the class. Compare the following:

> Take out your grammar **book**—Take out your work**books**
> Put your **hand** up if you know—**Hands** down!
> Pass your **essay** to the front when you've finished—Finish your **essays** off at home

4 ★ Put your desks *to their own places.*
Put your desks back in their places/where they belong.

1 **Hands up!**
Put your hand(s) up
Put your hand(s) up if you know the answer
Put your left/right hand up
Keep it up
All those who got it right, put your hands up
Up with your hand(s), if you know the answer
Those of you who know the answer, put your hand(s) up
I'm sorry, I thought you had your hand up
I keep seeing the same hands all the time

2 **Hands down!**
Hands down again
Put your hands down

3 **Open your desks**
Close/shut your desks
Put your schoolbag/satchel/bag away
Put it on the floor under your seat
Put your book in your desk
Put that away
Put your name/namecard up
Take out your namecard(s) and put it/them on your desk(s)

4 **Put your desks together**
Put/push your desks into groups of four
Could you give Bill a hand moving the desks
Turn your desk round (so that it faces the board/Bill)
Put your desks back where they were
Push your desks back (to) where they belong

1 • **Turn round** can be used for both a 90 and 180 degree turn. For a 360 degree turn you should say **turn right round** or **turn all the way round**.

1   **Turn round**
Turn right round
About face/turn!
Turn and face the board
Face the other way

2   **Look left**
Look to the left/right
Look straight ahead
Look straight in front of you
Close your eyes
Eyes closed!
No peeping
Face the front

3   **Hold up your pens**
Hold your books up
Put them down again
Put them back down

4   **Jump up and down**
Hop on one leg
Wave your hands
Wave your hands about in the air
Touch your head/toes
Point to your ears
Keep perfectly still
Don't move
Stay where you are

5   **Come on now!**
Get moving/cracking/weaving!
Buck up
Let's see some action then
Look lively
Don't hang about, get on with it
We haven't got all day
Stop dilly-dallying

1 ★ Look *here*.
This is really a threat in English, meaning something like: 'Now I'm going to show you!'

Similarly *listen here*.

●   **Look** can also precede a warning or command. It then suggests irritation:

> Look! Try not to make so much noise
> Look, John! I've had enough of that

'I will now explain the progressive methods by which your children are taught—so keep quiet, sit up straight and don't fidget.'

1 **Look this way**
Look at me
Look over here
Pay attention now
Could I have your attention, please
Try to concentrate now
Don't look out of the window
Eyes to the front, please
Face the front
Look up for a moment
I'm sorry to interrupt you, but could you look this way for a moment
Don't sit there daydreaming

2 **Be quiet!**
Everyone listen
Stop talking now
Stop chattering there
Ssshhh!
What's all this row/noise?
Don't make such a noise
Not so much noise, please
Don't all shout/talk at once
Listen to what I'm saying
Silence, please
Don't talk
Could I have a bit of quiet, please
Shut up, all of you!
Put a sock in it, will you
Don't bang/slam the lids of your desks
Could you sort it out after the lesson
Get on with your work quietly
Not another word, please

3 **Sit still**
Stand still
Don't move
Nobody move
Settle down, all of you
Everybody stay where they are
Stay where you are
Don't keep turning round
Turn this way
Turn round and face me
Stop fidgeting/messing about/playing the fool
Behave yourself!
Take your feet off the desk
Sit up (straight)
Don't be such a nuisance
Be a good boy/girl for once
Sit down
Stay in your seat

1 ● Notice the phrase 'some tasks for you to work **on** in pairs'. The preposition is essential.

'I strongly suspect you belong to an organisation that's diabolically opposed to Authority.'

3 ★ Everybody work *for* his own/*for* himself.
Everybody work on his own./by himself.

'Just say you brought him up on Spock—I've jotted the name down—and I'll throw him on the mercy of the Court.'

1 **Work in twos**
Work together with your friend
Find a partner
Work in pairs
Work in threes/fours/fives
Work in groups of two/three/four
I want you to form groups. Three pupils in each group
I'll divide the class into groups
Get into groups of three
Form two groups of six
Here are some tasks/exercises for you to work on in groups/pairs/threes
I want you to do some playreading in groups

2 **You'll have to join this group**
There are too many in this group
Bill and Alison, you can join group 3
There should only be three people in each group

3 **Work on your own**
Everybody work individually
Work by yourselves
Try to work independently
No cheating
Don't disturb your neighbour
There's no need to discuss it with your neighbour

4 **Do it like this**
Watch me first
Watch me doing it
Listen to me saying it
Copy me
Do what I'm doing
Do this
Do it this way
Like this, not like that
Try to do it exactly the same way as I'm doing it

1 ● These phrases simply mean 'stop' and do not suggest anger or irritation.

2 ● See Unit 4, section B.

3 ● These phrases are used where the pupil is doing something the teacher does not approve of. They are generally spoken in an angry tone and sound very different from similar expressions in 1, above.

'Nine years old and he doesn't even know how to manipulate his parents.'

5 ● These pedagogic sarcasms should be used with care.

1 **Stop now**
Everybody stop what they/you are doing
That's enough for now
That's fine
That will do, thank you
OK, that's enough
All right, you can stop now

2 **You will have to finish in a minute**
I'll have to stop you in two minutes
Your time is up now, I'm afraid

3 **Stop that!**
Stop it!
Stop doing that!
That'll do now!
That's enough of that!
No more of that!
Give it a rest!
Cut it out!
I've already asked you to stop once. I won't tell you again

4 **Leave it alone!**
Don't touch it!
Hands off!
Leave it where it is
It's fine where it is
Stop fiddling with the light switch

5 **I hate to interrupt your conversation, but . . .**
If you stop chattering, you might even learn something. You never know
Shall we try to behave like normal human beings for a change?
This is not a holiday camp/rock festival
I know the word 'work' may be new to you, but . . .

8 EXERCISES

I. Fill in the gaps, using the words or phrases below:

a) face	j) heads	r) referee
b) yourself	k) partner	s) three cheers
c) playing the fool	l) hand	t) fiddling with
d) your own	m) your marks	u) behave yourself
e) tune	n) get into	v) alone
f) word	o) keep the score	w) chattering
g) join in	p) all day	x) you three
h) peeping	q) draw	y) do now
i) with your back		

1. Try to do as much of the exercise as you can on … … without using a dictionary.

2. Could you give … me a … moving the screen out of the way. It's too heavy for me by myself.

3. Let's decide which team starts by tossing a coin. Right, Christos, … or tails?

4. I want you to … … three teams of six. That's the way.

5. Right, Andy, come out to the front and … the class.

6. John, you can be the … in this game. Make sure nobody cheats. And Alison, you … … …. The first team with five points is the winner.

7. Come on now, everybody close their eyes. And you, Tariq, no ….

8. What am I holding behind my back? I'll give … … guesses.

9. Well done, team A. You're the winners. Let's give them … … . Hip, hip, hurray!

10. Hey, you there! That book doesn't belong to you, does it, so please leave it ….

11. Look, Lee, try to … … or you can go outside. I mean it.

12. Carmen, put your book away. That's right. And do stop … … your pencil. Just put it on the desk. It won't walk away!

13. How about a song? Yes? Right. Well, you already know the … —it's the same as 'Clementine'—so you can … … with the group singing on the tape.

14. How many times do I have to tell you? Girls, stop …! You can talk during the break. Come on, I mean it. That'll … …!

15. Both teams got ten points, so it's a …. Well done.

16. Come here for a moment, could you, John. I'd like a … … with you about your homework.

17. Oi! You two boys. Stop … … … will you. How am I expected to teach with you two clowns in my class?

18. We'll work in twos now, so find yourself a …. Come on, hurry up. We haven't got … ….

II. Fill in the missing prepositions and adverbs in the following sentences.

1. Right. Now we'll start the game. … your marks, set, go!

2. No, Linda. I said 'Simon says "sit down"', so I'm afraid you're ….

3. Don't worry if you don't know the tune. I'll accompany you … my guitar.

4. Please try to work ... yourselves.

5. Could you put your desks back ... their places before you leave.

6. Well done, this team. Three cheers ... team 2!

7. This is a grammar exercise for you to work ... in pairs.

8. Stop talking now, and look ... here for a moment.

9. The first boy or girl ... the right answer will get a point.

10. We haven't got much time, so you will have to finish this ... two or three minutes.

III. Think of *two* appropriate phrases that you might address to the following pupils.

1. Gisela—is not paying attention.
2. Björn—is standing up.
3. Loizos—you can only see the back of his head.
4. Giorgio—finds it impossible to be silent for more than a minute at a time.
5. Delma—is not looking at the blackboard.
6. Ali—is attempting to become the first book juggler.
7. Vladislav—has got his feet on the desk.
8. Dan—is sprawled out across his desk.
9. Mahar—is disturbing the girl sitting next to her.
10. Vera—is copying the answers from somebody else.
11. Bekir and Salih—are arguing about something.
12. Hans—the slowest and dreamiest boy in the class.

IV. Try to check the answers to exercise II with a class that consists of the pupils described in exercise III.

V. a) Label the numbered objects and places in the sketch below.

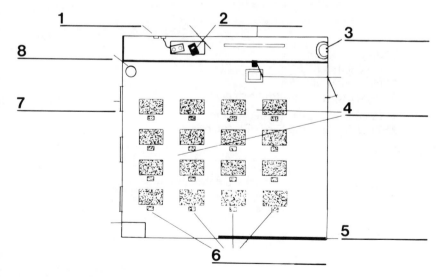

b) Now think of some appropriate instruction or warning connected with each of the objects/places mentioned. Use your imagination.

ANSWERS

I

1. your own
2. hand
3. heads
4. get into
5. a face
6. referee; keep ... score
7. peeping
8. you three
9. three cheers
10. alone
11. behave yourself
12. fiddling with
13. tune; join in
14. chattering; do now
15. draw
16. word
17. playing the fool
18. partner; all day

II

1. on
2. out
3. on
4. by
5. in
6. for
7. on in
8. over
9. with
· 10. in

III Suggested answers

1. Gisela, pay attention./Don't sit there daydreaming, Gisela.
2. Could you sit down, please, Björn./Stay in your seat, please.
3. Don't keep turning round./Face the front, would you.
4. Giorgio, be quiet and listen to what I'm saying./Not another word out of you, Giorgio, or else!
5. Delma, look at the blackboard./Eyes to the front, please.
6. Ali, please stop fiddling with your books./Leave your books alone, could you, Ali?
7. Take your feet off the desk, please./This isn't a rock festival, so feet off the desk now.
8. Sit up straight./Stop messing about, would you, Dan, and just sit up.
9. Just stop doing that, please, Mahar./Leave her alone.
10. Try and work on your own, Vera./No cheating, please.
11. Sort it out after the lesson, please./Put a sock in it, both of you. We're trying to do some work.
12. Come on now. Look lively!/Stop dilly-dallying, Hans. We haven't got all day.

V a)

1. the sockets
2. the register
3. the sink/wash-basin
4. an aisle/a gangway
5. the noticeboard
6. rows of desks
7. the window sill/ledge
8. the wastepaper basket/rubbish bin

b)

1. Come and plug the tape-recorder in.
2. Take the register to the staff room, please.
3. Go and rinse your hands under the tap.
4. Take your bag out of the gangway.
5. Go and stand by the noticeboard.
6. These two rows can be team 1 and these two rows team 2.
7. Take your books off the window ledge.
8. Throw it in the wastepaper basket.

Unit 9

'Yes?'

1 ★   Say it *loudly*.
       Say it louder./Speak up.

   ●   The verb 'say' must have some direct object. Check the errors in the following (answers at 5, below):
   ★   *Say louder.*
   ★   *Say again.*
   ★   *Say so that we all hear.*

   ●   The following verbs also require an object: **open, correct, leave, find.**

4 ★   Let's *take it* again.
       Let's try/say/do it again.

5 ●   It should be remembered that a whole sentence may be an unnatural reply.
       A phrase or even a single word is more common:

> Where is Mr Brown going?—He is going to London
> To London
> London

> Do you like football?—Yes, I like football a lot
> Yes, I do, a lot
> Yes, a lot

It should always be remembered that questions can be answered using
a completely different grammatical structure!

> Where is Mr Brown going?—He didn't tell me
> How should I know?
> Don't you mean Mrs?

> Do you like football?—I've never seen the point in it
> Give me cricket any day
> You're one of those cissy-types, are you?

Pupils need practice in recognizing the discourse links between sentences like
the above. Over-precise, grammatically complete replies may improve accuracy
but may also hinder the development of the listening skill.

   ●   Answers:

> Say **it** louder
> Say **it** again
> Say **it** so that we all hear

1 **Louder, please**
Speak up
Say it louder
Say it a bit louder, please
Once again, but louder
Say it so that everyone can hear you
I can't hear you. Say it again, but this time louder

2 **More clearly**
Speak more clearly
Not so quickly, I can't follow
Slowly does it!
Carefully does it!

3 **Not so loud**
Softer
There's no need to shout
I'm not deaf

4 **Again, please**
Once more
Once again, please
Say it again
Say it once more
Once again, but more fluently
Let's try it again
Again, but more quickly this time
Repeat, please
Repeat after me: 'It's a blue car'
Say after me: 'He has gone'
Say it after me

5 **The whole sentence, please**
Use a complete sentence
Begin with the question word
Try it again from the beginning

6 **Let her try it on her own**
Don't whisper the answer
Don't help him
I'm sure she can manage on her own
Don't keep prompting

1 ★   *Say everyone.*
 Everyone; everyone say it.

- The verb 'say' is tricky, and in fact you can often do without it:

> Everybody say it = Everybody/all together
> Say it louder = Louder/speak up
> Say it again = Again/once more

- *Say* and *tell* are sometimes confused:

SAY: *something (to somebody)*
       I'm afraid I've got nothing to say to you.
       something (to somebody) about something
       Could you say a little to us about your holiday?

       Idiomatic usage:
       Thank you. *I wouldn't say no to* another glass.
       I'm not sure, but *let's say* in about three weeks' time.
       We'll meet again in two months, *that's to say* in July.
       I'm quite willing to help. *Just say the word.*
       How long will it take?—*I couldn't say.* Perhaps an hour.
       There's no point doing this again.—Well, *if you say so.*

TELL: *somebody (about something)*
       Tell us about the end of the story.
       somebody (something)
       Don't tell me. I can't help you.
       Tell her what happened and why you came.
       somebody to do something
       Tell them to keep quiet.
       something to somebody
       Would you tell a thing like that to your best friend?

       Idiomatic usage:
       Tell the time/the truth/a lie/a story/the difference.
       Listen. *I'll tell you what.* We'll leave this till next time.
       It's *impossible to tell* which is which.
       It may rain tomorrow. *You never can tell.*

5 ● **Wait your turn.** No preposition is required.

1 **Everybody**
   Everyone, listen and repeat
   All together now, please
   Everyone, say 'She has gone'
   All of you
   The whole class, please
   Not just this row
   Let's read in chorus
   Let's all say it together
   Say it with me

2 **Boys—Girls**
   Now all the boys
   Just the girls
   Girls only
   Let's begin with the boys
   The boys can begin

3 **This row**
   The next group
   These two rows
   The back row on its/their own
   These tables on their own
   Just the front row

4 **In turns**
   One after the other, please
   In turn, starting with Bill
   Take it in turns, starting here
   Don't all answer together
   One at a time, please

5 **Your turn, Bill**
   Just you, Alison
   You on your own/by yourself, Alison
   Now you, Bill
   One boy at a time! The rest (of you), wait your turn
   Next one, please
   Now let's have someone else try it
   Not you again, Bill
   Don't let's leave it all to Alison

6 **You, too, Bill**
   You join in, Alison
   Join in with the rest of us, Bill

1 • Note the sequence of tenses:
I'll start and **you continue.**
You start and **I'll continue.**
The **you**-form is really an imperative.

★ Before you *will* answer.
Present tense after conjunctions **when, after, before, while**.

3 • When 'Sorry' means 'I didn't hear' the intonation is high rising. When it means 'I am sorry that I stepped on your toe', for example, it is generally low rising.

★ *How* was that?
What was that? See Unit 6, section D7.

The questions *how was that* and *how's that* would probably be used in the following situations:

He scored 45% but failed.—How's that? I thought 40% was the borderline. (= How is that possible?)

I'm looking for something in blue.—Well, how's that? It's quite cheap, too. (= Will that do?)

★ I *don't* hear.
I can't hear.

1 **I'll begin**
I'll ask first
I'll read first and then you can read after me
I'll start and you continue
I'll read the whole thing before you answer

2 **Now you ask Bill**
Ask Bill the same question
Now it's your turn to ask Bill
Now Alison, say to Bill: 'I'm very well'
Ask the boy/girl (sitting) in front of/behind you
Then you ask this boy, and he asks Bill and so on round the class
Now ask the boys and girls: 'Is it big or small?'
Now it's your turn to ask the question
Now it's Alison's turn to give the commands
You are the teacher now. Ask the class: 'What is this?'

3 **Sorry? What did you say?**
Sorry?
What?
Pardon?
What was that?
Speak up
I missed that. What did you say?
Sorry, I can't hear you
I didn't quite hear/catch what you said
The rest of you, keep/be quiet
I can't hear what Bill is saying for the noise
I beg your pardon. I thought you said: '. . .'

1 ● These phrases merely indicate that the pupil's answer was correct. 'Good' does not necessarily suggest a brilliant answer, just that the teacher is acknowledging what the pupil said.

● 'Uh-huh' and 'Hm-hm' should not be used too much.

2 ● These phrases can relate to (i) an action, or (ii) an answer.
   (i) If the pupil correctly carries out an instruction given by the teacher, e.g. holding his left hand up, opening his book at page 56.
   (ii) If the pupil correctly answers a question, e.g.:
   Teacher: Why is this sentence wrong?
   Pupil: The word 'has' is missing.
   Teacher: Yes, that's right.

That's the way also indicates approval and encouragement.

3 ● These phrases are rewards for outstanding answers, etc. Overused, they lead to inflation!

● Teachers may pay too much attention to the grammatical form of an answer and not enough to its communicative intent. Interesting exchanges develop:

> Pupil: 3,000 people died of starvation
> Teacher: Yes, very good

It is often extremely difficult to separate the pedagogic role (providing feedback) from the interaction role (providing opportunities for genuine communication).

● The following comments are often used on written work:

Excellent work	Satisfactory
Very well done	Could do better
Good stuff	Too many careless slips
Keep it up	Careless
Adequate	Needs to show more effort
Much better	Not up to your usual standard
Shows some improvement	Disappointing
Great improvement	See me about this

1 **Good**

Right	Yes
Fine	Right you are
Hm-hm	Quite right
Uh-huh	

2 **That's the way**

That's right	That's quite right
That's it	Yes, you've got it
That's correct	You've got the idea

3 **Excellent**

Very good	Magnificent
That's very good	Terrific
Well done	Wow!
Very fine	Jolly good
That's nice	Great stuff
I like that	Fantastic
Marvellous	

You made a very good job of that

4 **That's perfectly correct**

There's nothing wrong with your answer
What you said was perfectly all right
You didn't make a single mistake
That's exactly the point
That's just what I was looking for
I couldn't have given a better answer myself

5 **No, that's wrong**

Not really
Unfortunately not
I'm afraid that's not quite right
You can't say that, I'm afraid
You can't use that word here
Good try, but not quite right

6 **Could be**

It depends
It might be, I suppose
In a way, perhaps
Sort of, yes

1 • These phrases are used when the pupil improves at his second attempt.

2 ★ *Not yet.*
Not quite.

3 ★ Maybe this *helps* you.
Maybe this will help you.

'*O.K. Let's try again, but we don't have to hurry this time. We've got lots of time.*'

1 **That's better**
   That's more like it
   That's a bit more like it
   That's much better
   That's a lot better
   You've improved a little

2 **Try it again**
   Have another try
   Not quite right. Try again
   You were almost right that time
   Almost right
   Not exactly
   Well, err, . . .
   That's almost it
   You're half way there
   You're almost there
   You've almost got it
   You're on the right lines/track
   Take it easy
   There's no need to rush/hurry
   There's no hurry
   We have plenty of time
   Go on. Have a try
   Have a go!
   Have a guess if you don't know

3 **Don't worry**
   Don't worry about your pronunciation
   Don't worry about the spelling
   Not to worry, it'll improve
   Maybe this will help you
   What if I give you a clue?
   I'll help you if you get stuck

4 **You read quite well**
   You have very good pronunciation
   Your pronunciation is very good
   You sound very English
   You speak/read very fluently
   You have made a lot of progress
   You still have some trouble with your spelling
   You find it difficult to read aloud
   Reading aloud is difficult for you
   You need some more practice with these words
   You'll have to spend more time practising this
   You're getting better at it all the time
   You've improved no end

4 • It is clearly up to teachers to decide when such phrases are appropriate. Expressions of joy, sympathy, surprise, interest, etc., may also be equally effective:

> Good gracious! You were right!
> It must be my lucky day
> That is a very interesting suggestion, but . . .

1 **That wasn't very good**
That was rather disappointing
That wasn't up to much
Come on, now!
I wasn't very satisfied with that/the way you did that
That was awful/terrible/rotten

2 **You can do better than that**
Come on, can't you do any better than that?
There's room for improvement there all right!
Try harder
A bit more effort
Pull your socks up!
Come on, wake your ideas up
Put a bit of life into it

3 **I hope you do it better next time**
In future I want you to bring your workbook
When you try this again, I shall expect you to . . .
The next time we do this, I want you all to . . .
From now on there will be no interrupting
This is the last time I shall tell you

4 **You fool!**
Idiot!
Nincompoop!
You buffoon!
Nitwit!
You stupid idiot!
I've never heard anything so ridiculous!
What a load of rubbish!

1 • See Unit 6, section D1.

2 ★ *Has everybody the possibility to see?*
Can everybody see?
Avoid the phrase 'have the possibility', as it is often incorrect.

Notice: Is there any possibility of you(r) finishing this at home?
There's always the possibility of using the passive.

3 • See Unit 6, section D4.

'Fortunately for him he has the best left hook in the School.'

4 • Notice some of the uses of the word 'trouble':

Verb:
Don't trouble to write out the whole exercise
Could I trouble you to turn the lights off?
What troubles me is that you're making the same mistakes

Noun:
What's the trouble? Is it too difficult?
The trouble is that you're not really trying, are you?
You've **taken a lot of trouble over** this work. Good
Are you sure you want to do it?—Yes, **it's no trouble** at all
You're asking for trouble if you go on making that noise

1 **Has everybody got a book?**
Is there anyone without a book?
Who hasn't got a copy of the text?
Where is your workbook, Bill?
Is there anyone who hasn't got a copy of the article?
Can anybody lend Bill a copy of the book?
Would someone give Alison a sheet of paper?

2 **Can you see all right?**
Can you see the picture?
Can you hear all right?
Can you all see/hear?
Is the volume all right?

3 **Have you found the page?**
Is there anybody who still hasn't found the page?
Have you all found the place?
Help him find the place
Show him the place
Show him where we are

4 **Who needs help?**
Who can't manage (on his/her own)?
Does anybody need any help?
Is anyone having trouble/difficulty?
Who is having trouble with this exercise?
Who is finding this difficult?
How are you getting on/along?
I'll help you if you get stuck
Let me know if you run into a problem

5 **Have you all prepared this chapter?**
Did you all finish off this exercise at home?
Have you all completed the essay, as I told you?
Have any of you not made a list of questions?

6 **All of you try**
What's the matter?
What's the problem?
Why don't you join in?

1 • Questions like 'Where was I?' the teacher probably addresses to himself. Alternatives in this situation include:

> Let's get back to what we were doing
> To continue what I was saying, . . .
> To pick up where I left off, . . .

Notice also:

> By the way, . . .
> While I am thinking/think about it, . . .
> While I still remember, . . .
> While we're on the subject, . . .

3 ★ *You were already.*
You have already had your turn.

Already, yet, still and *ever* cause problems:

Already: We've already done this exercise.

In negative and interrogative sentences, *already* suggests surprise:
Have you already finished?

Yet: Generally in negative and interrogative sentences; final position:
Has anyone finished yet?
We haven't checked this exercise yet.

Still: Often corresponds to *yet* but in mid position:
We still haven't checked this exercise.

But notice:
Do you still find these exercises easy?
Do you find these exercises easy yet?

Ever: Generally in negative and interrogative sentences or where doubt or a condition is expressed:
Do any of you ever listen to the BBC World Service?
If you ever have time, it's worth listening to.

1 **Where did we stop last time?**
How far did we get last time?
Where did we finish/stop reading last time?
What were we talking about last time?
Let me refresh your memory. Last time we talked about . . .
If I remember correctly/rightly, we were on page 20
Last time we got to line 15
If you can recall what I said last time about . . .
Let's revise some of the things we did last time
Where was I?
What was I saying before I was interrupted?
What were we talking about before Marco came in?

2 **Are you ready?**
Who has finished?
Who has done them all?
Are you all ready now?
Have you all finished?
Anybody not finished?
Have you finished, Bill?
Have you done exercise 7 (yet)?
Have you finished reading page 10?
Anybody who still hasn't finished?
Have you done everything?
How far have you got?
Which question are you on?
Where are you up to?

3 **Who's next?**
Whose turn is it next?
Who is the next one to try?
Your turn
You next
Now you
You're next
Who hasn't had a turn?
Who else is there?
Who's left?
Who hasn't been out to the board?
You have already had a turn
You have been out once already

1 • Notice the colloquial reduced questions without a verb:

> Any volunteers to help me?
> Anybody willing to read the part of Jack?

Such phrases require a rising intonation.

★ Who *comes* and *writes* that for me?
Who will/wants to come and write that for me?

'*For her free choice she wants traditional structured learning.*'

1 **Who wants to come out?**
  Who would like to do this?
  Who wants/would like to write that on the board?
  Who'll write that up on the blackboard?
  Who wants to be Mrs Brown?
  Any volunteers to read (the part of) Sherlock Holmes?
  Who would like to read the part of John?
  Who'd like to be the reader?
  Who wants to change the pictures?
  Anybody willing to clean the board for me?
  Is there anybody interested in carrying the projector?
  If nobody is willing, then I'll have to choose somebody

2 **Which English name do you want?**
  Which name would you like (to have)?
  Do you want to be John or Mark?
  Which name do you like best/prefer?

3 **Which team do you want to be in?**
  Do you want to be in Bill's team?
  Which group would you like to join?
  Is there anybody in particular you would like to work with?

4 **Which topic would you like to take?**
  Which subject do you want to work on?
  Is there a particular topic you are interested in?

5 **It's up to you**
  You can decide/pick/choose
  I'll leave it up to you to pick your topic
  It's all the same to me which group you join
  It makes no difference (to me) which exercise you do
  I don't mind either way

9 N PROGRESS IN WORK

1 • These phrases are for catching attention. They indicate that one particular activity has finished and that another is about to be explained.

2 • When the teacher explains what is about to happen, he must use the **future tense.** The only exceptions are modal verbs. Check the errors in the following (answers at 6, below):
   ★ *Now we sing a song.*
   ★ *Now I give you a little test.*
   ★ *Soon we hear your story, too, Meg.*

3 ★ Now *we take* the dialogue.
   Now we'll listen to/do the dialogue.

   ★ 'At first' is almost always wrong in a classroom situation. 'At first' always implies a contrast:

   | At first I liked him, but later I hated him |

   • Notice the word order possibilities with 'first' and 'first of all'.

4 ★ And *then*, exercise B.
   And now (for) exercise B.

6 ★ 'At last' is almost always wrong in a classroom situation. It implies longing and anticipation:
   At last we have finished this stupid book!

   • Answers:

   | Now we'll sing a song
   Now I'll give you a little test
   Soon we'll hear your story, too, Meg |

1 **Right**
Good
Fine
OK
All right
Okey-dokey

2 **Now we shall do some groupwork**
Now let's have a look at exercise 13B
Now I want you to turn to page 17
How about listening to the whole thing now?
Now we can relax
Now I have some music for you

3 **First of all, we shall . . .**
First, let's listen to the dialogue
Firstly, a few words about your homework
To begin with, we shall do some drills
Let's first listen to Mary's dialogue
We can look up the new words first of all
The first time, you can try it with your books open

4 **Next, I would like you to . . .**
For the next thing, could you take out your workbooks
And now a brief look at some grammar
First, . . . then we shall do it in pairs
After that, you can change roles
After each part, you can check the answers
When you have done that, you can continue with number 3

5 **Now we'll go on**
Let's move on to something different
Let's turn to something a little less serious for a moment
Before we go on to chapter 10, let's . . .
Let's stop here for a while
I think we can leave it there for a while
We can come back to this exercise a bit later
If we could just go back to the last chapter

6 **Finally, I want you to . . .**
To finish (off) with, you can do some reading
For the last thing today would you take out your notebooks
Last but not least, we have a radio programme to listen to
Finally, a brief word about next Monday
Firstly . . . secondly . . . and lastly, I want you to . . .
Just before we finish/you go, could I . . .

1 ★ This type of phrase is a frequent source of error, mainly because of the word 'so':
 ★ Now we do *so that* Dieter is the teacher and . . .
 ★ Now I want you to read *so that* the girls are Mrs Smith and . . .
 The correct version involves either (i) a participle phrase, or (ii) a preliminary sentence:

> (i) Now we'll try it **with Dieter playing** the teacher and . . .
> Now I want you to read **with the girls reading** Mrs Smith's part and . . .
> (ii) **This is the way we'll do it:** Dieter is the teacher and . . .
> **I want you to do it like this:** the girls can be Mrs Smith and . . .

The most natural use of 'so that' in English expresses purpose:

> Stand aside **so that** we can all see the board
> Try to be here early **so that** we can start on time

 ● The verb 'explain' requires 'to' before the indirect object:

> Can you explain this sentence to us?

 ★ Not: Can you explain *her* why it is false?

3 ● *Do* and *make* are often confused. Notice the following selection of idioms and uses:

DO	MAKE
Do this exercise at home	How many mistakes did you make?
Do your homework	Can you make yourself understood?
You're doing very well	Does it make sense to you?
Try to do your best	Make the sentences plural
Are you going to do French next year?	This makes quite a difference
Do question 17	What time do you make it?
It has nothing to do with you	Make groups of 6
You could do with some practice	You've made a lot of progress
It isn't good enough. It won't do	You'll make a good player one day
	I'll make this the last question today

Consult the *Oxford Advanced Learner's Dictionary of Current English* for further examples. See also exercise iv of this unit.

1 **This is the way we'll do it**
This is how we shall do it
I would like you to do it in the following way:
Could you do it this way/like this:
Try to do it the way we did it last time
Do it the same way as last time
What we shall do is this:
Let me explain what I want you to do:
Before you begin, let me tell you how I want you to do it
This time we'll do it with Maria reading

2 **The idea of this exercise is to . . .**
The idea behind this is for you to ask questions
The idea is that you use the conditional
The purpose of this is (for you) to practise the future
What this exercise is trying to do is (to) make you think
The point of the second exercise is for you to ask me some questions
Are you all clear about what you have to do?
Are there any questions?

3 **You can spend ten minutes on this**
I'll give you until ten past to finish this off
You have five minutes to complete this
You'll have to stop in two minutes/minutes' time
Don't spend more than a few minutes on/doing this

'Sid, I wish you wouldn't bother trying to explain the offside rule.'

9 EXERCISES

I. Fill in the gaps, using appropriate words or phrases from the following list.

a) a clue
b) more like it
c) no end
d) manage
e) prompting
f) volunteers
g) brief word
h) speak up
i) that's the way

j) wait your turn
k) had a turn
l) room for improvement
m) row
n) get stuck
o) right lines
p) getting along
q) up to much
r) missed

s) made a slip
t) refresh my memory
u) we got
v) willing
w) either way
x) run into
y) easy
z) go

1. Don't all shout at once. Please ... ...

2. Once again, please. I'm afraid I ... what you said.

3. Last time we were talking about pollution. What did we say. Can anyone ... ...?

4. That was one of the best essays I've ever read. It was a pity that you ... ... in the very last sentence.

5. Go on. Have a try! I know you can do it. Have a ...!

6. No, not like that, Yutaka. Try again. Yes, that's ... ...

7. I'm afraid I didn't catch the last word. Could you ... .

8. Just before you go, a ... ... about Monday's test.

9. And the next sentence, please. No, not you again Kemal. You've already ... ...

10. This exercise isn't as easy as I thought. Is there anybody who can't ... ...?

11. Right. Let's finish off the chapter. Does anybody remember how far ... ... last time?

12. There's no need to rush. Just take it ... and try again.

13. All right. Everybody stand up. Now look at the door. ... ... Now turn round and face the window.

14. There are four topics to choose from and the first one is 'America between the Wars'. Any ... for that one?

No? Isn't anybody ... to try it? It's quite interesting.

15. Come on, I said repeat after the tape. Oh dear, that wasn't ..., was it? Try again. Well, there's still plenty of ..., I'm afraid.

16. Your answer wasn't quite right, but you're definitely on the ....

17. I could hardly believe my eyes when I read your essay. It was really good. You've improved ... since last year. Well done!

18. The second half of the exercise is quite tricky, so if you ... let me know and I'll come and help.

19. It makes no difference to me whether you write it in pencil or in ink. I really don't mind ....

20. If you ... any problems, just put your hand up and I'll come round and try to help.

II. Re-express the sentences, using the preposition or adverb given in brackets.

| Example: Could you say it louder, please. (UP)
| Could you speak up.

1. I want you to try to do exercise 5A on your own. (BY)
2. Let's read the passage. One at a time, starting with John. (IN)
3. You're making too much noise and I can't hear. (FOR)
4. This work wasn't as good as you usually do. (UP)
5. How far have you got? (UP)
6. Do you understand what you have to do? (ABOUT)
7. You seem to find spelling difficult. (WITH)
8. I'll let you choose which subject you write about. (UP)

III. Complete the sentences, using the words given in brackets and any other extra words (prepositions, pronouns) necessary to make a correct sentence.

1. Take out your books and ... ... (OPEN/PAGE 73)

2. That was a good try, Françoise, but I don't think you would ... ...
   (SAY/ENGLISH)

3. Could you speak up a little. I'm afraid I ... . (NOT/HEAR)

4. If I remember correctly, in the last lesson Bekir ... ... the energy crisis in
   the West. (TELL/SOMETHING)

5. What you said sounded fine, but could you ... ... (SAY/LOUDER)

6. Last time you seemed to ... ... use the conditional tense.
   (FIND/DIFFICULT)

7. I'll read out some sentences and your job is ... ...
   (WRITE/DOWN/NOTEBOOKS)

8. Now, whereabouts is Liverpool? Georg, would you like to come and ... ...
   (POINT/OUT/US)

IV. Fill in the gaps, using the correct form of either 'do' or 'make':

1. I'm afraid you ... ... several mistakes in this exercise. You had better ... it again.

2. Is there anybody who hasn't ... his homework? Good. And what about exercise 9?
   Did any of you ... that as well?

3. I ... it almost ten to ten and we have finished everything we planned to ... this
   morning. We have ... very well.

4. Everyone seems to be ... progress with their projects. At least, you all seem to
   be ... your best with them.

5. Could you ... three groups of five, please. Hurry up, boys, ... up your mind which
   group you want to join.

6. How many of you … German as well as English? I see. That … quite a difference.

7. We'll try and … the drill we started last time. Remember, in this exercise you have to … the questions and the answers will be on the tape.

8. There's no need to … questions 6 and 7. They don't seem to … much sense, and I don't think they really have anything to … with this chapter.

9. The idea of this exercise is to … the sentences passive. Could you … this work in your exercise-books first, please, and … any you don't finish now at home.

10. I don't want to … you … this again, but several of you could … with some extra practice. Let's … number 9 the last one for today, though.

V a) Read through the extracts from lesson plans. Then try to explain what you are going to do, using the various phrases listed in section N4.

Example:

> 1. Look at homework
> 2. Start Unit 9

First of all, we'll have a look at your homework and then we'll go on to Unit 9.

1

> 1. Read paragraph 2
> 2. I - ask questions on text
> 3. Try exercise 10A

2

> a) Exercise 19A
> b) Read through answers
> c) Write out in notebooks

3

> A. Vocabulary work
> 1. 2 write words on board
> 2. They copy down

4

> 3. Exercise 7 (1-5 only)
> 4. Oral!
>
>   Then write answers.

5

> 6. Chapter 9 - if not finish, leave till next time.
> 7. Song - 1. Listen + follow from OHP 2. Join in.

6

> Tests
> 1. Go through answers
> 2. Count up points.
> 3. See if score over 30/40

V b) Now give explanations for the following extracts. This time check the phrases listed in section N5.

Example:

> 1. Read conversation again
>   (Bill = Mr Jones)

Now we'll read the conversation again, but this time with Bill reading Mr Jones' part.

7

> 1. Practise telephone
>   conversations
>   (girls = answering the phone
>   boys = ringing up)

8

> 1. Dictation
>   (same as last time)

9

> 7. Tests
>   Explain: 1. Listen tape /once
>   only
>   2. Answer questions
>   (tick right alternative)

10

> Groupwork
>   Explain how — in pairs
>   — A ask questions
>   — B answers
>   — change over

11

> 6. Exercise 10B
>   Explain idea: practise
>   asking questions
>   politely.

12

> 11. Fill in policeman's part
>   (5 minutes only!)
>
> 12. Any questions?

VI. Think of some suitable comment to make to the pupils in the situations below. Notice: Q = difficulty of question; P = ability of pupil; R = result.

Example: Q—very difficult; P—average; R—correct
Comment: Well done/Excellent

	Q	P	R	Comments
1.	Average	Average	Correct	Pupil asked to pretend to be airline passenger
2.	Very diff.	Average	Good	Encouraging
3.	Difficult	Good	Very good	Perfect answer
4.	Difficult	Average	Wrong	Encouraging
5.	Average	Good	?	Encouraging
6.	Easy	Average	Good	Second attempt
7.	Average	Weak	Good	Improvement
8.	Difficult	Average	Wrong	Almost
9.	Easy	Average	Poor	Grumbling
10.	Very diff.	Average	?	Guess

VII. Fill in *yet*, *already*, *still* or *ever*.

1. Have you finished ...? That was quick.

2. If you ... use this phrase, please remember that it is very colloquial.

3. OK, so much for grammar. Aah, just a minute. We ... haven't checked the exercise you did as homework.

4. Haven't you finished ...? You are slow.

5. If I remember correctly, we've ... done the first half of the exercise.

6. That just leaves questions 6–10 ... to do.

7. You're not supposed to start answering .... Wait until you hear the signal.

8. Any questions? Is there anybody who ... doesn't understand what he or she has to do?

9. Your spelling is very careless. Have you ... tried using a dictionary to check it?

10. If you haven't ... checked your answers, I'd like you to start doing it now.

VIII. Find a lesson plan containing a variety of activity types. Begin and end each stage of the plan. Make the transitions naturally and remember to explain the purpose and give the duration of the activity.

IX. Choose a fairly difficult structure or vocabulary exercise and get your fellow students to give oral answers. Confirm or correct what they say. Encourage them, moan at them. Alternatively, organize a general knowledge quiz.

ANSWERS

I

1. wait your turn
2. missed
3. refresh ... memory
4. made a slip
5. go
6. that's more like it
7. speak up
8. brief word
9. had a turn
10. manage
11. we got
12. easy
13. that's the way
14. volunteers/willing
15. up to much/room for improvement
16. right lines
17. no end
18. get stuck
19. either way
20. run into

II Suggested answers

1. *by* yourself/ves.
2. Let's take it *in* turns to read.
3. I can't hear *for* the noise.
4. This work wasn't *up* to your usual standard.
5. Where are you *up* to?
6. Are you clear *about* what you have to do?
7. You seem to have trouble/difficulty *with* spelling.
8. I'll leave it *up* to you (to choose) which subject you write about.

III

1. open them at page 73
2. say it like that in English/say that in English
3. can't hear/didn't hear (you)
4. told us something about
5. say it louder
6. find it difficult to
7. to write them down in your notebooks
8. point it out to/for us

IV

1. made; do
2. done; do
3. make; do; done
4. making; doing
5. make; Make
6. do; makes
7. do; make
8. do; make; do
9. make; do; do
10. make; do; do; make

V Suggested answers

1. For the first thing today, I'd like you to read through paragraph 2. After that I'll ask you some questions on it. When we've done that, we'll go on to exercise 10A.

2. To begin with we'll do exercise 19A, and then we'll read through the answers. And finally I'd like you to write it out in your notebooks.

3. Now we'll do some vocabulary work. I'll write the words on the board and then you can copy them down.

4. For the next thing I want you to do exercise 7, but only the first five questions. First of all we'll do it orally and after that you can write the answers.

5. We can come back to chapter 9 next time. And now a song. First of all, just listen and follow the words from the transparency. Then I want you all to join in.

6. To finish off with let's have a look at your tests. Firstly we'll go through the answers, and then I'd like you to count up your points and see if you've scored over 30 out of 40.

7. Now we'll practise some telephone conversations, and we'll do it with the girls answering the phone and the boys ringing up.

8. For the next thing we've got a dictation, and we'll do it the same way as last time.

9. Now we have a test. Let me explain what I want you to do. First, you must listen to the tape. You'll hear it once only. After that you must answer the questions by ticking the right alternative.

10. Now we'll do some groupwork, and this is how I want you to do it. You work in pairs with one person asking the questions and the other answering. After that, you can change over.

11. Now we can move on to exercise 10B. The idea of this exercise is for you to practise asking questions politely.

12. What I want you to do is to fill in the policeman's part. I'm afraid you can only spend five minutes on this. Are there any questions?

VI Suggested answers

1. That's the way./You've got the idea.
2. Very good indeed./Terrific.
3. That's just the answer I was looking for./I couldn't have given a better answer myself.
4. Good try, but not quite right./I'm afraid that wasn't quite right.
5. Could be./It depends.
6. That's more like it./That's a lot better.
7. You've improved no end./That was much better.
8. You've almost got it./You're on the right track.
9. Can't you do any better than that?/Come on now, that wasn't up to much.
10. Have a guess if you don't know./Go on, have a try.

VII

1. already	6. still
2. ever	7. yet (already)
3. still	8. still
4. yet	9. ever
5. already	10. already

Unit 10

P Language Work

The word 'MTish' refers to the mother tongue of the learners, for example, for Spanish learners:
What's the Spanish for 'car'?

1 ★ Mistakes are very common with phrases of this type. Spot the errors in the following (answers at 4, below):
★ *How* is the MTish for 'car'?
★ *How* is this sentence in MTish?
★ *How* do you call this (thing) in English?

See also Unit 6, section D7.

'*Has phar la houdla seel vo plate?*'

'*Glhup hwow you shoul do da?*'

4 ● Answers:

> **What** is the MTish for 'car'?
> **How** would you **say** this sentence in MTish?
> **What** do you call this (thing) in English?

1 **What's the MTish for 'car'?**
What's the MTish word for 'car'?
What's this sentence in MTish?
How would you translate this word/phrase into MTish?
How do you say this/'on the wall' in MTish?
What do you call this thing in English?
What is the English equivalent of the MTish word 'Feierabend'?
How would you say that in English?

2 **Please translate**
Translate this/that (last sentence) into English
Could you put that into MTish for us
Translate from MTish into English
Don't translate word for word
Think about the meaning of the whole sentence

3 **In English, please**
Say it in English, please
Use English
Try it in English
Now the same thing in English
This is supposed to be an English lesson, so let's speak English

4 **It's almost the same in English**
The English word is almost the same
The English for this is very similar

1 • Teachers say 'let's talk about this chapter' and they really mean 'let me ask you some questions'. A more honest phrase would be: **Let's look at this chapter in more detail.**

★ Let's discuss *about* this.
Let's talk about this.
'Discuss' is not followed by a preposition. It is also rather inappropriate in the classroom.

2 ★ *I think you haven't* had this word. See Unit 4, exercise II.

★ We *handled* this verb last time.
We dealt with/did this verb last time.
Notice also:
Last time we saw how the conditional is/was formed.
In the last lesson you saw how Alan Harris escaped from prison.

★ Let's *pick up* the new words.
Let's look at/pick out the new words.

3 ★ Mistakes are frequent with this type of phrase:
Say *otherwise* 'he returned'
Say *in another way* '— —'
Say *in other words* '— —'
Say *in two words* '— —'
Say this *shortly*
Identify the mistake and correct. (Answers, below at 5.)

• Notice the pattern:

What is	another a better a shorter a more English	way of saying '— —'?

4 • **Say, tell, speak** and **talk.** Compare the correct and incorrect versions of the following sentences:

★ He *told* he was going	He told **me** he was going
★ He *told about* his trip	He told **us** about his trip
★ He *talked something* about a holiday	He **said** something about a holiday
★ He *spoke nothing* to me about it	He **said** nothing to me about it
★ *What* are you *talking?*	What are you talking **about**?
★ Let's see what our book *tells*	Let's see what our book **says**

5 • Answers:

How else could you say 'he returned'?
What is another way of saying '— —'?
Can you **say the** same **thing** in other words?
What are two words that mean (the same as) '— —'?
What's a shorter way of saying this?

1 **Let's talk about this chapter**
Let's see if you've understood
Let's ask some questions about/on this passage
Who is going to ask the questions about/on page 123?
You had the job of preparing five questions each on this unit

2 **We'll have a look at the new words**
I don't think you've had/met this word before
Let's read through the vocabulary first
I think we had this verb last time
We looked at/dealt with these forms last week
You had this in your last lesson

3 **What's another way of saying 'he stuttered'?**
How else can you say the same thing?
Can you say the same thing, using different words?
Give a synonym for 'rushed'
What is a synonym for 'huge'?
Another phrase/expression that means the same thing
What's another word that means the same as 'huge'?
What are two words that mean the same as 'tripped'?
Can you give me one word that means 'to come back'?
What's one word that means/for 'out of work'?
What's a shorter way of saying 'he went by plane'?
Give me a phrase that means approximately/more or less the same thing

4 **Use your own words**
Use your own words to describe what happened
Use your own words to tell me about John
Explain the meaning of this sentence, using your own words
Tell me in your own words what happened
Can you paraphrase/summarize the last paragraph?
Can you give me the main ideas of the passage in a nutshell?
Give me a brief summary of the contents

5 **What does 'blue' mean here?**
In what sense is the word 'cry' used here?
What does it mean in this context?
What does 'sang' refer to in this sentence?
What do the words in brackets/italics mean here?

3 • Check that you know the alphabet in English and can use it fluently.

A	[ei]	J	[dʒei]	S	[es]
B	[bi:]	K	[kei]	T	[ti:]
C	[si:]	L	[el]	U	[ju:]
D	[di:]	M	[em]	V	[vi:]
E	[i:]	N	[en]	W	[ˈdʌblju:]
F	[ef]	O	[ou]	X	[eks]
G	[dʒi:]	P	[pi:]	Y	[wai]
H	[eitʃ]	Q	[kju:]	Z	[zed]
I	[ai]	R	[a:]		

Notice: Ä—A with two dots (over it)
      Å—A with a little O (over it)
      Ø—O with a stroke through it

★ *One letter is too much.*
There is one letter too many.

• An 'a' *in* the beginning. In identifying the position of a mistake, remember:

at the beginning
at the end
in the middle

4 • Check the following vocabulary:

,	comma	?	question mark
.	full stop	!	exclamation mark
;	semi-colon	'	apostrophe
:	colon		[əˈpɔstrəfi]
-	hyphen [ˈhaifn]	" {	inverted commas
	(e.g. passer-by)	{	quotation marks
.—	dash	()	brackets
	(e.g. we—that is I—...)	*	asterisk
/	stroke		

1 **How do you spell 'buses'?**
How do you spell the word 'glass'?
How is 'giraffe' spelt?
What is the correct spelling of this word?
Spell 'ship' for me
Spell it aloud
Spell it in English
Use the English names for the letters

2 **Have you spelt it right?**
Let's see if you've spelt it right/correctly
I wonder if you've spelt it right
Is there anything wrong with the spelling?
Can anybody correct Bill's spelling?
I'm afraid this is spelt wrong
I'm sorry, you've made a spelling mistake
There are two words you've spelt wrong
You've slipped up over/on two words

3 **What letter is missing?**
Is this letter right/correct?
Spell it with an 'i' and then an 'e'
There's a 'k' missing
A 'k' is missing
'K' is missing
There's one letter too many/few
You've got one 'l' too many/few
It's spelt with two 'p's, not one
Double 'k'
You need an extra letter here
There should be an 'o' instead of a 'u'
Write it with a capital 'J'
Spell it with small letters
The word ends/begins with the letter 'p'
It begins with a 'j'
It's spelt the same as in MTish
Why do you need two 'o's?
Why should there only be one 's'?
Write it as one word/two words
Write it separately/together
These two letters are the wrong way round
The word is spelt 'c-o-n-s-c-i-o-u-s'

4 **You need a comma here**
There should be a full stop
Put a comma after this word
Always check the punctuation
Can we leave this comma out?

1 ★   Can you say *so*?
    Can you say that/it like that?
    But compare: A: How do you know it's true?
                    B: Well, Jim said so.

2 ★   You *did* a mistake.
    You made a mistake/slip/error.

  ★   *A* wrong tense.
    The wrong tense. There is a tendency to use the definite article with 'wrong'.

3 ★   *How do you say it better?*
    What's a better way of saying it?

'*Brain like a computer—keeps making fantastic mistakes.*'

1 **Is that right?**
What is the answer?
Was that the correct answer?
Can you say that?
Can you say it like that?
Think about it carefully. There's a catch (in it)
It's a trick question
Don't fall into the trap

2 **You made a mistake**
You made a small/slight mistake
You made a little slip
There was a small mistake in what you said
That wasn't quite right
That was almost right—just one little slip
You missed the verb out
You forgot the preposition
You used the wrong tense
You misunderstood the instructions

3 **How should you say it?**
What should you say?
How should you answer?
What would you say, Bill?
Did anyone notice the mistake?
Can anyone improve on that/what Alison said?
Is there anything to correct/that needs correcting?
Anything wrong in sentence 3?

4 **Is there another way of saying it?**
Is there a better/shorter way of saying the same thing?
What's a better way of saying it?
That is all right, but is there another way?
Any alternative suggestions for number 6?
Can anyone say it another way?
Try to put it in other words
Could you phrase it slightly differently
What other word could you use here?
What else could you say?
How else could you say it?

5 **That's another possibility**
That's one answer I hadn't thought of
I hadn't thought of it that way
That's an interesting suggestion
It had never struck me that it could mean that
That's one way of looking at it

1 ★   Can we leave this *away*.
  ● **Can we leave this out/miss this out.**
    See Unit 7, exercise I.

       Notice also: You have to **include** the preposition
                    The preposition has to be **kept in**

4 ● Notice the prepositions:

> to be derived **from**
> to correspond **to**
> the opposite **of**
> similar **to**
> to be based **on**

1 **Can we leave this out?**
Is a relative pronoun necessary here?
Do we need the relative here?
Which tense do we use after 'if'?
Which preposition comes after 'to concentrate'?
What preposition does 'to be proud' take?
What's the rule about 'some' and 'any'?
Does anybody remember the rule for using 'since' and 'for'?
Does anybody recall what we said about the verb 'to dare'?
What's the past (tense) of 'to go'?
What are the parts of 'to sing'?
Where do we usually put adverbs of frequency?
Is the word order right?
Where does the word 'yet' usually come?

2 **Try it again**
Now ask properly
Again, but this time more politely/fluently/clearly
Once again, but remember the word order
This time start with 'who'
Watch out for the conditional tense this time
Mind the preposition
Put the adverb at the end
Try not to mix these two words up
Don't get 'skirt' and 'shirt' mixed up
Don't be misled by the Swedish word
They're spelt the same, but pronounced differently

3 **It sounds better to say '. . .'**
What you said isn't wrong, but . . .
Perhaps you had better say . . .
It might be better to say . . .
I think 'then he left' sounds better in this sentence
An Englishman would probably say . . .

4 **What is the noun derived from 'electric'?**
What is the verb that corresponds to this noun?
What's the adjective that comes from 'nation'?
What's the opposite of 'generous'?
What is the prefix that means 'against'?
A word that rhymes with 'blue' meaning 'a hint' or 'tip'
It's a synonym of/for 'jealous'
What's a man who carries bags called?
What do you call a person who moves to another country?
What's the difference between 'stick' and 'racket'?
Can anyone tell me the corresponding verb?

1 ★   *Listen me* saying it.
     Listen to me saying it.

Whenever the verb 'listen' is followed by an object, the preposition 'to' is required:

> Listen **to the tape**
> Listen **to me**
> Listen to **John saying it**
> Listen to **how I say it**

Note also:

> Listen!
> Listen carefully!
> Listen again

'Listen here' usually precedes an angry threat or piece of advice:

> Listen here. I'm fed up with this noise.
> Just listen here. If you say that again . . .

1 **Listen again and say it after me**
It wasn't pronounced correctly
There was a mistake in the pronunciation
Again, please, but watch your pronunciation
Be careful with the 'sh'-sound
You said 'class'. Listen to the correct pronunciation
You are saying 'tree'. I'm saying 'three'
Listen and repeat
Listen to me saying it
Listen to the way I say it
Listen to how I say it
Listen again carefully and then you try

2 **Listen to the way my voice goes up**
Watch my lips very carefully
Watch my mouth closely
Notice how my tongue touches my teeth
See how my mouth hardly moves
The man on the tape raised his voice like this
You try and do the same
You must let your voice fall at the end of the sentence

3 **The word is pronounced** [hou'tel]
The word rhymes with 'house'
The word is accented on the second syllable
The first sound is [θ], as in 'thin'
Don't mix up these two words, 'glass' and 'class'

1 • These sample instructions illustrate the typical form of instructions in English. Any standard textbook will have additional examples, e.g. W. Stannard Allen, *Living English Structure*, Longmans, 1959.

★ Put the sentences *into passive*.
   Put the sentences **into the passive.**
   Articles required with parts of speech and grammatical categories. See also Unit 6, exercise III.

• Notice the prepositions:

> Change **A into B**
> Put **A into B**
> Substitute **A for B**
> Replace **A by/with B**
> Form **A from B**

2 • Notice the pattern:

> Fill in the gaps, **using** the words given ⇒ Use the words given **to** fill in the gaps

'If he'd only teach us something useful!'

1 **Change/put into/form/rewrite**
   Put the sentences into the passive/into direct speech
   Put the verb into the correct tense
   Rewrite the sentences, using the passive
   Rewrite the following sentences, leaving out the relative
   Rewrite the sentences in the singular/in indirect speech
   Rewrite the passage, correctly punctuated
   Rewrite in the first person
   Change all nouns into pronouns
   Substitute 'too' and 'enough' for 'so' in these sentences
   Rearrange the adjectives in the correct order
   Write the verbs in brackets in their correct form
   Change these sentences in the same way as the example
   Replace 'which' with 'that'
   Make these sentences passive
   Form adjectives from these nouns

2 **Fill in/complete/insert/expand/supply**
   Complete the sentences with a suitable infinitive
   Complete the sentences by adding an article
   Fill in 'a' or 'the' where necessary
   Complete the sentences, using the words provided
   Use one of the following words to complete the sentences
   Construct a suitable completion for the sentences
   Use appropriate forms of 'to be' to complete the sentences
   Insert the words given in brackets into the sentences
   Fill in the gaps/blanks, using the words given
   Put 'shall' or 'will' into the blank spaces
   Supply the correct form of the verb
   Supply the missing word
   Add the correct endings
   Fill in the missing speeches in the following conversation
   Supply the missing articles
   Expand the notes below into complete sentences

3 **Play the part of the librarian**
   Take the parts indicated
   Each group represents one political opinion
   Take turns to make offers and then refuse them
   Study your role and then work out a conversation
   Take on the roles of the people you heard in the dialogue
   Act as an interviewer and ask members of the class if they . . .

1 ★   ... that fits *to* each sentence.
        'Suit' and 'fit' require no preposition here. Notice the following:

> This suits me fine
> It's **suitable for** me
>
> The shoes do not fit me
> His plan does not **fit in with** ours
> This beer is not **fit to** drink

●   Notice the pattern:

Cross Ring Underline Mark Tick	the right answer ⇒
Cross Ring Underline Mark Tick	the right answer ⇒

Put a	cross over/on/by ring round line under mark by tick by	the right answer

1 **Choose/cross/underline/ring/find**
Choose the verb that best fits each sentence
Choose the correct alternative
Choose the correct completion for each sentence
Ring the appropriate answer
Put a ring round the best alternative
Underline the accented syllable in these words
Put a line under the correct preposition
Cross the appropriate answer
Put a cross in the right box
Find words in the text that mean (the same as . . .)
Find English words that mean the same as . . .

2 **Construct/write/make/combine/continue**
Construct sentences using the words given
Write sentences to explain the following words
Write appropriate answers to the following questions
Write out the following numbers in full
Make sentences to show you understand the meaning of the following words
Combine each pair of sentences, using 'although'
Continue the conversation between Fred and Tom
Finish the dialogue

3 **Write/summarize/explain/punctuate**
Write an essay of about 250 words on one of the following subjects
Write an answer to Bill's letter. Begin: 'Thanks for . . .'
Summarize the passage in not more than 100 words
Read the following passage and then answer the questions on it
State Bill's reasons for leaving in your own words
Explain the meaning in English of the following words
Explain the meaning of the following words, as used in the passage
Punctuate the following passage

4 **Now talk about yourself in the same way**
Continue in the same way
Now say what you enjoy doing, using the ideas below
Now ask for and give opinions on the following topics
Now offer these people some advice
Use these ideas to practise similar conversations
Now you make some suggestions. Begin 'How about . . .?'
Talk about yourself. You may find these ideas useful

1 • These phrases may be used after a pupil has given his opinion or mentioned some facts. They help to make the exchange more natural and provide a link with the next speech or question.

2 • These questions are to be used as a follow-up to 'yes/no' answers or to statements.

 ★ Why do you think *so*?
 The word 'so' cannot be emphasized in this context. Generally, in such a sentence, 'why' would be emphasized, or sometimes 'think'. English requires the use of **this** or **that** to express emphasis:

> I see. But why do you think **that**?
> Yes, but why did you write **this**?

 • Notice the following useful reaction devices:

 1. Pupil: They shouldn't get married too young.
 Teacher: What exactly do you mean by too young? Sixteen? Twenty?
 2. Pupil: It has always been cheaper to travel by ship.
 Teacher: But that doesn't mean to say it'll be cheaper this year.

3 • The phrases in these sections help to keep the conversation moving.

5 ★ *Has anybody of you anything to say?*
 'Anybody', 'somebody', 'nobody' and 'everybody' cannot be used with 'of':

any of you		Has anybody anything to add?
some of you		Somebody must know the answer
all of you	but	Everybody will have to finish this off at home
each of you		
none of you		Nobody managed to get them all right

1 **I see**
   Oh, did you/is it/was there/can they?
   That's interesting
   What you said is very interesting
   I didn't know that
   Is that so?
   Really?
   Fancy that!
   That's a very good point
   I hadn't thought of that
   Yes, that's true, as a matter of fact

2 **Why?**
   In what way?
   How?
   Why do you think so?
   What reasons do you have for saying that?
   Can you support what you say?
   Is there any evidence to support what you say?

3 **Do you really think so?**
   Is that your honest opinion?
   Is that what you honestly think?
   You're convinced of this, are you?
   Don't you think, though, that . . .
   I'm not so sure about that
   Well, that all depends, doesn't it?
   You can't be serious

4 **I'm not sure what you mean**
   I'm not sure what you are getting/driving at
   Could you explain what you mean
   Could you give me an example
   What exactly are you trying to say?
   Could you go into more detail
   Could you expand on that a little
   Be a little more precise. What exactly do you mean?
   You mean, then, that . . .
   Correct me if I'm wrong, but do you mean that . . .

5 **Has anybody else anything to say on this?**
   Have you got anything to add (to what Bill said?)
   Who agrees/disagrees with Bill/what Bill said?
   Does anybody share Bill's opinion/views?
   Bill, what do <u>you</u> think about this?
   Could someone sum up what has been said
   Let's just run through the arguments for and against
   Perhaps we could come back to what Gino said earlier

I. Fill in the gaps, using 'how' or 'what':

1. ... is the Finnish for 'journey'?

2. ... should you say this word?

3. ... is another way of saying 'he starved to death'?

4. Can anyone tell me ... you call a person who gives blood?

5. Do you remember ... you say in this situation?

6. ... is your answer to number 7, Daniel?

7. ... does the last one go, then?

8. ... have you written the last word?

9. ... would you say that sentence in English?

10. ... do you call the police in an emergency in England?

11. ... do you think, Ali? ... does this sentence sound to you?

12. ... have you answered number 6? ... have you written?

13. ... does Mr Brown's new car look like? Petra ... do you say?

14. ... is the answer to number 25? ... is the sentence in Turkish?

15. ... else could you say this? ... would you say, Ricardo?

II. Make oral corrections or guide the pupils to the correct answer, using the following spelling and grammatical errors.

1. The boy is **kiking** the ball.
2. He is **hopeing** to become a reporter.
3. They play **foot ball** in **juni**.
4. There is a **bicture** on the **wal**.
5. The dog is **pihainta** table.

6. They depend very much **from** the price.
7. I was **at seven o'clock at the club**.
8. If you **would have come,** you would have enjoyed it.
9. This is the book **which I buyed**.
10. We started reading it **for three weeks ago**.

III. Spell out the following nonsense messages, using the names of the letters and punctuation marks.

1. W?V:QAER!
2. IH/GY*()J.
3. "EI-RGJ;WY'

IV. Fill in the appropriate forms of 'say', 'tell', 'speak' or 'talk' in the following sentences:

1. So far we have … nothing about the Marshall Plan, although last time we … about American involvement in Europe, and I … you that it really began after World War II.

2. … up! I can't hear what you are … . … everybody what Mr Brown … to the shopkeeper. … English, please!

3. Stop … now! I'll … more slowly if you can't follow. I don't think we have … anything yet about this chapter. John, perhaps you could … us something about it?

4. We'll have to … this idea over next week. We haven't … much about it so far, but I'll see whether the headmaster has anything to … about it. By the way, could you … me the time, please.

5. To … the truth, this wasn't an easy exercise, but as you didn't … anything about it, I guessed it was all right. It's almost impossible to … the difficult exercises from the easy ones until you do them yourself.

V. Choose the correct completion for each sentence on the left from the list on the right.

A. What is another way	1. for 'car'
B. What is the opposite	2. into the passive
C. Which verb corresponds	3. into English
D. What is the Turkish equivalent	4. of saying this sentence
E. How would you translate this	5. of 'exciting'
F. What's the M tish	6. by pronouns
G. Put all the verbs	7. to the speaker, Mr Brown
H. How would you say that	8. for the word 'and'
I. The pronoun 'he' refers	9. in English
J. Replace the nouns	10. to the noun 'terror'
K. Substitute relatives	11. from the noun 'symbol'
L. This adjective is derived	12. of 'sauna'

VI. The passage below is being dealt with by means of vocabulary questions. The teacher's notes under the passage show the type of question he or she asked. What were the questions?

> and hesitated momentarily before boarding the crowded train. He looked back anxiously and thought he caught a glimpse of the scarlet hat that had so terrified him in Rome after Nino had escaped. He had jumped at the opportunity of two weeks in Italy, but he had been required to risk his neck, let alone that of his closest friend, for a story that might never appear. It would, of course, be replaced by his obituary.

Example: terrify ⇒ adjectives: terrific, terrible

What are the adjectives that are derived from the verb 'terrify'?

1. momentarily = for a moment
2. crowded = full of people
3. to catch a glimpse of = to see
4. scarlet = MT translation
5. jumped at the opportunity = when he was given the chance, he did not hesitate at all
6. to risk one's neck = MT translation
7. story = here: newspaper article
8. obituary = MT translation
9. anxious ⇒ noun: anxiety
10. It would, of course, be replaced by his obituary. It = the story he was looking for.

VII. The following items are taken from sample exercises. What instructions were written (or given orally) for these exercises?

1. Q: Last week I ... to London. (go)
   A: Last week I went to London.
2. Q: They drink a lot of coffee in Finland.
   A: A lot of coffee is drunk in Finland.
3. Q: I want to show you a book. I bought it last week.
   A: I want to show you the book I bought last week.
4. Q: ... United States, ... Great Britain and ... Soviet Union.
   A: The United States, Great Britain and the Soviet Union.
5. Q: I | like chocolate, but Bill | like lemonade.
        | likes | likes
   A: I <u>like</u> chocolate, but Bill <u>likes</u> lemonade.
6. Q: a) because he needed the money
      b) because he felt lonely
      c) because he had a new typewriter
   A: b)
7. Q: banana; hotel; education
   A: ba<u>na</u>na; ho<u>tel</u>; edu<u>ca</u>tion
8. Q: The boy is playing with the ball.
   A: He is playing with it.

9. Q: I wanted to see his red/famous/new bicycle.
   A: I wanted to see his famous new red bicycle.
10. Q: I enjoy pop-music. But I don't buy records.
    A: Although I enjoy pop-music, I don't buy records.
11. Q: 21/6/72.
    A: The twenty-first of June, nineteen seventy-two.
12. Q: I have just had my breakfast, so I am not ....
       a) angry b) hungry c) thirsty d) sleepy
    A: b) hungry

VIII. Fill in the gaps, using an appropriate word or phrase from the following list.

a) in a nutshell   i) substitute
b) catch   j) mixed up
c) slipped up   k) take
d) struck   l) word for word
e) paraphrase   m) worthwhile
f) evidence to support n) correspond to
g) context   o) sum up
h) dealt with   p) phrase

1. Number 5 was very difficult indeed. I think you all ... ... on this one.

2. Yes, that is possible, I suppose. It had never ... me that it could be an adverb here.

3. You're right. It does mean 'crazy' usually, but it means 'angry' in this particular ....

4. Don't use the same words as the girl in the passage. You must ....

5. You want to know the rules. All right, here they are ... ... Just the main facts.

6. Now you've heard a lot of interesting arguments in support of this idea. Would someone like to ... ... what has been said so far?

7. As far as I remember we ... ... the use of 'since' and 'for' last time, but some of you are still getting them ... .

8. That's right. He was very proud, but not 'to his car'. What preposition does proud ...?

9. This isn't really a trick question, but there is a slight ... in it. The thing is not to translate it ... ..., but just give the general idea.

10. I think it'd be ... trying this again, but this time try to ... the last sentence a little differently.

IX. React to the following statements made by pupils during a conversation lesson. Try to think of two appropriate reactions for each statement.
 1. 'I thought it was a terrible film.'
 2. 'The number of accidents went down last year.'
 3. 'One solution would be to ban traffic from the city centre.'
 4. 'There are several countries where this is already done.'
 5. 'What we want is some kind of music censorship.'
 6. 'A lot of drivers go far too fast.'
 7. 'Nuclear power is the only answer. Anyway, that's what I think.'
 8. 'Another idea would be to limit the number of foreigners coming into the country.'
 9. 'Petrol will soon become too expensive. Last year, for example, the price per litre went up by 15%.'
 10. 'Clearly, men are much better drivers than women. Everybody knows that.'

X. Organize and run a conversation on the following topics.

1. School discipline
2. TV serials
3. Fashion
4. People who keep pets
5. Teacher training

Remember to react to comments appropriately and keep the conversation moving.

XI. Work in fours. Each group has a selection of tests or essays written by older pupils and containing several mistakes. Each person takes it in turn to explain the mistakes to the others.

ANSWERS

I

1. What	6. What	11. What; How
2. How	7. How	12. How; What
3. What	8. How	13. What; What
4. what	9. How	14. What; What
5. what	10. How	15. How; What

II Suggested answers

1. Which letter is missing? There's one letter missing.
2. There's one letter too many.
3. Write 'football' as one word. 'June' is spelt with a capital 'J', and there should be an 'e' instead of an 'i' at the end.
4. The word begins with a 'p', not a 'b'. You need a double 'l' here.
5. 'Behind the' is written as two words. There should be a 'b' instead of a 'p'. Is this 'a' correct? The word ends with 'd'—'behind'. 'The' is spelt 't-h-e'.
6. Which preposition comes after 'to depend'?
7. Is the word order right? Does anybody remember what we said about the order of adverbs?
8. Which tense do we use after 'if'?
9. Do we need the relative here? What is the past tense of 'to buy'?
10. What is the rule about 'for' and 'ago'?

III Check answers from section P3, page 204.

IV
1. said; talked; told
2. Speak; saying; Tell; said; Speak
3. talking; speak; said; tell
4. talk; said; say; tell
5. tell; say; tell

V

A—4	G—2
B—5	H—9
C—10	I—7
D—12	J—6
E—3	K—8
F—1	L—11

VI Suggested answers
1. What's another way of saying 'momentarily'?
2. What are three words that mean the same as 'crowded'?
3. Can you give me one word that means to 'catch a glimpse of'?
4. What's the MTish for 'scarlet'?
5. Explain the meaning of this sentence, using your own words.
6. How would you translate 'risk his neck' into MTish?
7. In what sense is the word 'story' used here?
8. What is 'obituary' in MTish?
9. What is the noun that comes from 'anxious'?
10. What does 'it' refer to in this sentence?

10 ANSWERS

VII Suggested answers

1. Complete the sentences, using the correct form of the verb given in brackets./ Supply the correct form of the verb.
2. Make the sentences passive./Rewrite in the passive.
3. Combine the sentences, using a relative pronoun where necessary.
4. Fill in 'a' or 'the', where necessary./Fill in the missing articles.
5. Choose the correct form of the verb./Underline the correct form of the verb.
6. Cross the appropriate answer./Choose the correct alternative.
7. Underline the accented syllables in the following words.
8. Change all nouns into pronouns./Rewrite, using pronouns.
9. Rearrange the adjectives in the correct order.
10. Combine each pair of sentences, using 'although'.
11. Write out the following date in full.
12. Complete the sentences, using one of the words given./Choose one of the following words to complete the sentences.

VIII

1. c   6. o
2. d   7. h, j
3. g   8. k
4. e   9. b, l
5. a   10. m, p

IX Suggested answers

1. Did you?/In what way?
2. I didn't know that./Yes, that's true, as a matter of fact.
3. Could you go into more detail?/I hadn't thought of that.
4. Could you give me an example?/Be a little more precise. What exactly do you mean?
5. You can't be serious./Is that what you honestly think?
6. What exactly do you mean by far too fast? 80 kph? 100 kph?/What do you mean exactly by a lot of drivers? 10%? 50%?
7. Who agrees with what X said?/Has anybody else anything to add on this topic?
8. I'm not so sure about that./Correct me if I'm wrong, but do you mean that we should not allow foreigners to visit our country?
9. Yes, but that doesn't mean to say it'll go up by 15% this year./That's a very good point.
10. Is there any evidence to support what you say?/Does anybody share X's view?

APPENDIX: PUPIL LANGUAGE

This section contains a list of phrases that post-intermediate pupils might be expected to use during an English class. Shorter phrases (e.g., **good morning, thank you**, etc.) are listed in the relevant sections of Units 3–10. See index.

1. Following the Lesson

Repeat
I'm sorry, I didn't understand
You're speaking too quickly
I didn't get that down. Could you say it again?
Could you repeat the last bit?
I missed the beginning of what you said
Could you explain again, please?

Explain
I don't understand what I'm supposed to do
Do you mean that we should . . .?
When you said . . . did you mean that we should . . .?
Could you repeat the instructions, please?
Shall we do the exercise in our workbooks?
Are we supposed to finish this off at home?
What shall we do when we've finished?
What do we have to do next?
Can you help me, please?

Media
It's too loud/soft
I can't see/hear/follow
You're in the way
Could you write it up on the blackboard, please?

Place
Is it my turn?
Am I next?
Shall I start
Which number are we on/up to?
Where are we (up to)?

2. Correctness of Answers

Answers
What was the answer to number 7?
Could you read out the answer to number 3 again?
Was the answer to number 2 a or b?

Right/wrong
Why can't you say . . .?
Can I say . . .?
Is this a mistake?
What's wrong with (saying) . . .?
Why was what I wrote wrong?
Why did you mark this wrong?
Why did you put a line under this word?
Why was alternative b wrong? In the passage it says . . .
Isn't there a mistake in sentence 3?
Shouldn't there be an article?
Shouldn't the verb be in the future?
I think you've made a mistake on the blackboard

APPENDIX

3. Language Questions

Spelling
How do you spell . . .?
Are there two 'l's or only one?
Do I need a hyphen/comma/full stop?

Pronunciation
How do you pronounce the next word?
I'm not sure how to say the next word.
What's the next word?
Where's the accent in this word?

Grammar
Which tense do I need/should I use?
Why do you need the article?
Do you have to have an article?
What's the preposition after 'to depend'?
Could you use the future/passive here?

Understanding
I don't understand this word/the last word (on line 5)
Could you explain the meaning of this word?
What's the meaning of 'nuclear'?
I didn't understand what the first sentence meant.
I've never heard that word before
It still isn't clear to me what this means
Does it mean the same as . . .?
Is it more or less the same as . . .?
What's the MTish for this word?

Finding words
Is there a shorter way of saying this?
Is there a better way of saying the same thing?
What would be another way of saying it?
Is there a word in English that means the same as . . .?
Is there an idiom in English that corresponds to the MTish . . .?
What's the adjective derived from this word?

4. Politeness

Apologies
I'm sorry I'm late; I've been to . . .
I'm sorry, I don't know
I'm afraid I've left my book at home

Requests
Could I leave ten minutes early/
at twenty to?
Could I have another copy?
Have you got an extra sheet?
May I go to the toilet/lavatory?

Offers of help
Shall I turn the lights out?
Shall I draw the curtains?
Do you want a hand with the
table/moving the desk?
Can I help?